DATE DUE		

JAMES BALDWIN

LIVES OF NOTABLE GAY MEN AND LESBIANS

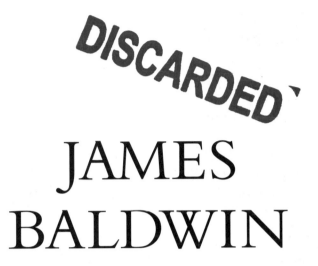

JAMES
BALDWIN

RANDALL KENAN

MARTIN B. DUBERMAN, General Editor

CHELSEA HOUSE PUBLISHERS ◼ New York • Philadelphia

CHELSEA HOUSE PUBLISHERS

EDITORIAL DIRECTOR   Richard Rennert
EXECUTIVE MANAGING EDITOR   Karyn Gullen Browne
COPY CHIEF   Robin James
PICTURE EDITOR   Adrian G. Allen
ART DIRECTOR   Robert Mitchell
MANUFACTURING DIRECTOR   Gerald Levine
PRODUCTION COORDINATOR   Marie Claire Cebrián-Ume

LIVES OF NOTABLE GAY MEN AND LESBIANS
SENIOR EDITOR   Sean Dolan

Staff for JAMES BALDWIN
EDITORIAL ASSISTANT   Mary B. Sisson
PICTURE RESEARCHER   Pat Burns
SERIES DESIGN   Basia Niemczyc
COVER ILLUSTRATION   Bradford Brown

First Printing

1 3 5 7 9 8 6 4 2

Library of Congress Cataloging-in-Publication Data

Kenan, Randall.
James Baldwin / Randall Kenan; introduction by Martin Duberman.
p. cm.—(Lives of notable gay men and lesbians)
Includes bibliographical references and index.
Summary: Describes the life of the writer James Baldwin, focusing on his experiences as an African-American civil rights worker and as a gay man.
ISBN 0-7910-2301-X
      0-7910-2876-3 (pbk.)
1. Baldwin, James, 1924–1987—Biography—Juvenile literature. 2. Afro-American authors—20th century—Biography—Juvenile literature. 3. Civil rights workers—United States—Biography—Juvenile literature. 4. Gay men—United States—Biography—Juvenile literature. [1. Baldwin, James, 1924–1987. 2. Authors, American. 3. Civil rights workers. 4. Gay men—Biography. 5. Afro-Americans—Biography.] I. Title. II. Series.
PS3552.A45Z75 1994   93-22776
818'.5409—dc20   CIP
[B]   AC

CONTENTS

Titles to come in

Reclaiming
the Lesbian and Gay Past

Martin Duberman

Being different is always difficult. And yet those of us who are different in size, shape, color, nationality, or sexual orientation should be delighted that we are *not* average, not just another cookie-cutter product of mainstream culture. We should glory in the knowledge that many remarkably creative figures, past and present, lived outside accepted norms and pressed hard against accepted boundaries.

Unfortunately, many of us have internalized the majority's standards of worth, and we do not feel very good about ourselves. How could we? When we look around, we see that most people in high places of visibility, privilege, and power are white, heterosexual males of a very traditional kind. That remains true even though racism and ethnocentrism have ebbed *somewhat* and people of diverse backgrounds have begun to attain more of a foothold in our culture.

Conforming to the prescribed model of what a person "should" be has historically been easier for some gays than for others. Those who looked and acted like "ordinary" people, instead of appearing "sissy" or "butch," could choose to "stay in the closet" and thereby avoid detection and social condemnation. These days, however, more and more gay people, sensing that the consequences are no longer as severe as they once were, *are* coming out. Yet there are still comparatively few role models for them to emulate.

Unlike other oppressed minorities, homosexuals can rarely find alternate sources of confirmation and worth within their own families. Even when a homosexual child is not rejected outright, acceptance comes within a family unit that is structurally heterosexual; the gay or lesbian teenager remains an exotic, unable to find in his or her family's traditions—as other minority people often do—a compensatory source of validation for the deprecations

7

of mainstream culture. Things are rarely any easier at school, where textbooks and lessons are devoid of relevant information about homosexuality. Nor does the mainstream culture—movies or television, for example—provide young gays and lesbians with accurate images of themselves, let alone any sense of historical antecedents.

This series is designed, above all, to fill that huge, painful cultural gap. It is designed to instill not only pride but encouragement, the kind of encouragement that literature and biography has always provided: proof that someone else out there has felt what we have felt, experienced what we have experienced, been where we have been, and has not only endured and survived but made important contributions.

A worthy goal, but how best to achieve it is problematic, particularly as regards *who* to include in the series. Categorizing human beings on the basis of sexual orientation is a relatively recent phenomenon of the last several hundred years. It is a development, many historians believe, tied to the increasing urbanization of Europe and the Americas, and the new opportunities city life presented for anonymity and for freedom from the relentless scrutiny of family and neighbors that had characterized farming communities and small towns. Prior to, say, 1700, it had been generally assumed that all human beings harbored erotic impulses toward both genders, even if acting on same-gender impulses was usually taboo. Indeed, in many non-Western parts of the world, it is still unusual to categorize people on the basis of sexual orientation alone.

But in the West, where we currently *do* divide humanity into separate, oppositional categories of *gay* and *straight,* most people grow up accepting that division as natural and dutifully assign themselves to one category or the other. But for a variety of reasons, many still refuse to define themselves as gay or lesbian. In some cases, they regard their sexuality as too fluid to fit into narrow, either/or categories. In other instances, while recognizing that their sexuality does fit within the gay category, they resist adopting a stigmatized public identity. In still other cases, the individual's sense of her or his sexual identity changes over the course of a lifetime, as does the sense of the importance of sexuality in defining who they are.

Complicating matters still further is the fact that even today there is no agreed-upon definition of what constitutes a gay or lesbian identity. Should we call someone gay if his or her erotic desire is *predominantly* directed toward people of their own gender? But then how do we measure predominance? And by *desire,* do we mean actual behavior—or fantasies and impulses that are never acted out? Some scholars and theorists even argue that genital sexuality need not be present in a relationship before we can legitimately call it gay or lesbian, stressing instead the central importance of same-gender *emotional* commitment. If we fall back on *self-*definition as the central criterion, that would, for the purpose of this series, force us to eliminate those historical figures who lived before *gay* or *lesbian* were available categories for understanding and ordering experience.

In deciding which individuals should be featured in *Notable Gay Men and Lesbians,* I have juggled, combined—and occasionally even finessed—these competing definitions. For the most part, I have settled on those figures who *by any definition*—same-gender emotional commitment, erotic fantasy, sexual behavior, *and* self-definition—clearly qualify for inclusion. And I have regretfully omitted many bisexual figures whose erotic and emotional preference seems indeterminable (most often for lack of documentation).

Although I have omitted most of these contested figures—for example, Margaret Mead, Janis Joplin, Judy Garland, and Billie Holiday—I have included a few, such as Marlene Dietrich, as witnesses to the difficult ambiguities of sexual definition, and to allow for a discussion of those ambiguities. In any case, the problems inherent in putting together this series pale in comparison to the satisfaction of being able to provide today's young gays and lesbians with a continuum of experience and achievement into which they can place themselves and lay claim to happy and productive lives. ▧

ALWAYS HIMSELF

Martin Duberman

James Baldwin lived and labored under the double burden (and blessing) of being black *and* gay. About his blackness he could do little—other than lift his uniquely eloquent voice in testimony to the daily humiliation of black American life and in celebration of its special virtues. About his gayness, he could do somewhat more. He could acknowledge—at a time when most Americans, black and white, did everything they could to hide from such truths—that the label "homosexual" did accurately describe most of his erotic impulses.

Yet at the same time, Baldwin did not feel that any one label could do justice to the actual complexity of his feelings. "Homosexual, bisexual, heterosexual are 20th century terms which, for me, really have very little meaning," he explained once to an interviewer. "I've never . . . watching life, been able to discern where the barriers were."

Baldwin's experiences ranged from one-night pickups with men to falling in love and living for a year with a young black woman to lifelong romantic friendships with people of both genders. Though, for public consumption, he never provided much detail about his private life, in his writing he was forthright, seeking always to "bear witness" to the truth of his experience. Indeed, his novel *Giovanni's Room* was one of the very first and most nuanced fictional treatments of homosexuality to appear in print.

As an adult, moreover, Baldwin was never shy about announcing his homosexuality to new acquaintances, figuring any relationship would profit from being truthful at the outset. To Baldwin, "love is love"—too rare a commodity to corrupt with deceit and equivocation. The gender of two lovers, he felt, was far less important than the fact of their love.

Baldwin suffered for his honesty and outspokenness. His searing words about the plight of black Americans made him a despised figure to many political conservatives, and his defense of same gender love discomforted even many of those who thought of themselves as liberals. Indeed, his own publisher rejected the manuscript of *Giovanni's Room,* and civil rights leaders, nervous about his homosexuality, excluded him from the roster of speakers at the 1963 March on Washington.

To Baldwin, such hostility typified American society's inability to acknowledge how intricate and undefinable human emotion and attraction can be—to say nothing of its fear of male intimacy and of egalitarian relationships. But Baldwin refused to bow to the dictates of others. He insisted always on being himself, even as he recognized that this "self" was changeable and in flux, and could never be fully encompassed by any single definition or label. ▨

CHAPTER ONE

INTO THE FIRE

He was terrified.

It was Monday, October 9, 1963, and James Baldwin had come to Selma, a small city in Dallas County in the south-central part of the state of Alabama, to help black Americans register to vote.

As had been taking place in Selma and elsewhere in the Deep South for decades, the right of black Americans to vote was being denied them through the use of a variety of unfair, illegal, and sometimes violent tactics, and despite such legal guarantees as the 15th Amendment (ratified in 1870) and the 1957 Civil Rights Act, both of which explicitly stated that the right to vote could not be denied anyone because of their race, color, or creed.

But in order to vote, one had first to register to do so with the proper authorities. By the early 1960s in the South, where, since the end of the Civil War and the release of blacks from legal bondage, whites had used terror, economic oppression, and the ruthless exercise of political power to prevent blacks from

Baldwin addresses a crowd of civil rights demonstrators in Montgomery, the state capital of Alabama, in the early 1960s. "I want to be an honest man and a good writer" was how Baldwin often described his goal in life.

claiming their constitutional rights, whites had become increasingly desperate to keep blacks from the ballot box.

For the previous decade or so, beginning with the U.S. Supreme Court's 1954 decision in *Brown* v. *Board of Education of Topeka, Kansas,* which struck at the very basis of segregation (the South's system of separating the races, based on laws and practice) by declaring that "in the field of public education, the doctrine of 'separate but equal' has no place," blacks had become increasingly insistent in their rightful demands for the justice that had been so long denied them, and it seemed at last that progress might be made. Although *Brown* applied specifically only to public education, its broader implications were clear. "Separate but equal" was the legal doctrine on which the entire southern system of segregation depended. Legally, states and local governments had been able to maintain separate public facilities for blacks and whites so long as those facilities were equal. In practice, separate but equal was a legal fiction; black facilities were never the equal of white facilities, as *Brown* and a series of prior Supreme Court decisions had come to recognize. In *Brown* the Court had gone even a step further: in education, the eight justices had unanimously ruled, separate but equal was "inherently" discriminatory. That is, even if the facilities were equal, the very fact of separation made their existence as segregated institutions legally indefensible. Applied to other aspects of public life, such logic would in the long term, as outraged white racists immediately recognized, sound the death knell of segregation.

As blacks, in the wake of *Brown,* organized for the purpose of challenging segregation in other aspects of public life, whites vowed defiance, and the question of voting rights—a tangible means whereby blacks, who constituted a significant portion of the South's population (in many places even an outright majority), could exercise the political power long denied them—became increasingly critical.

But as increasing numbers of blacks attempted to register to vote, white supremacists challenged them with every weapon at their disposal. Black Americans who tried to register were often fired by their white employers. They were verbally abused or set upon and attacked by angry mobs. They and their families were threatened with physical harm, often by policemen. (These threats were not idle; the bombing of black homes and churches by segregationists became virtually commonplace during the civil rights movement of the late 1950s and 1960s.) Activists and community leaders, especially those encouraging blacks to vote, were jailed on trumped-up charges, beaten, shot at, and even murdered.

Elaborate schemes were enacted to prevent blacks from participating at the polls. Voter registries were opened only at odd and extremely limited times—for one varying two-hour period once or twice a month, say, which was never announced in advance, and inevitably in the middle of a working day, a time when black access to the books would be limited. Those who gained access to the registration books were subjected to a literacy test—twenty-some questions, requiring a fairly sophisticated knowledge of the Constitution, U.S. history, and American jurisprudence. Whereas white voters were generally asked to do nothing more than read a line of the Constitution aloud and sign their name, blacks in Alabama, for example, were asked to "understand and explain any article of the Constitution of the United States to the satisfaction of the registrars." (In Selma, prospective black voters were asked, "what two rights does a person have after being charged by a grand jury?" and were disqualified for failing to cross a *t* on registration forms.) Those whom the registrars deemed had passed the examination were then required to pay a poll tax before they could actually register. In many jurisdictions, the amount of this tax for one year—not insignificant in itself—was multiplied by the number of years that had passed since the prospective voter had first been eligible to register. For example, a 38-year-old black would-be voter, inspired by the civil rights movement to register and somehow succeeding in his attempt, would be required to pay 17 years' worth (the amount of time elapsed since he first, at attaining majority at the age of 21, became eligible to vote) of poll taxes before he could actually cast a ballot. Needless to say, the accumulated cost was often prohibitive for blacks, most of whom occupied the lowest rungs of the South's socioeconomic ladder. For decades, most blacks had simply ceased trying to register.

The city of Selma, birthplace of the White Citizens Council, a supremacist group dedicated to the preservation of segregation, was notorious for its opposition to black voter registration. Early in 1963, 32 black schoolteachers there were dismissed from their jobs for having had the audacity to appear at the courthouse in an attempt to register to vote, and when blacks held a voter-registration rally at the Tabernacle Baptist Church, the city's infamous sheriff, Jim Clark (whose feelings about desegregation were succinctly expressed—"NEVER"—on the button he always wore on the lapel of his gold-braid uniform), led a posse of several hundred white men, armed with clubs, bullwhips, and cattle prods, to menace the gathering. Only 335 of the town's approximately 15,000 eligible black voters—a number that would have given Selma's blacks a majority in the town of 26,000—were registered to vote.

For these reasons, the Student Nonviolent Coordinating Committee (SNCC), a civil rights organization dedicated to peaceful protest, targeted Selma for a black voter registration drive, and James Forman, the executive secretary of SNCC, invited the famous author, speaker, and activist James Baldwin to join him and his young colleagues in their work there. Throughout the South, the members of SNCC were using the tactics of nonviolent protest—marches, boycotts, sit-ins—to challenge the status quo and to focus the attention of their fellow Americans, largely through the news media, on their just grievances and on the outrageous conduct and attitudes of the white southerners protecting the indefensible position of segregation, thereby eventually provoking, it was hoped, the federal government to action.

Through the presence of James Baldwin, the SNCC leaders could guarantee a high level of national interest in the events in Selma that October, for by the early 1960s the best-selling author had become internationally renowned for his eloquent, complex literary explorations of the tangled racial and sexual prejudices and illusions—not unrelated, in the author's mind—with which America was struggling. In three novels—*Go Tell It on the Mountain* (1953), *Giovanni's Room* (1956), and *Another Country* (1962)—Baldwin had, with a growing and unprecedented boldness, engaged in an increasingly forthright discussion of the history, prejudices, and fears that seemed to make genuine love—between races, and between individuals of either sex—so elusive, if not impossible, becoming in the process the first major American novelist to examine sexual love between males with any significant degree of candor and insight. From Baldwin, the causes and consequences of racial and sexual oppression had received their most profound fictional exploration to date.

His three books of essays—*Notes of a Native Son* (1955), *Nobody Knows My Name: More Notes of a Native Son* (1961), and *The Fire Next Time* (1963)—had cemented Baldwin's reputation as America's foremost literary spokesman for civil rights. In language unparalleled in its eloquence, insight, passion, and moral force, *Notes of a Native Son* and *Nobody Knows My Name* bore witness to the corrosive effects of American society on the emotional and intellectual development of a young black man. Even so, their considerable literary merit and commercial success were relatively insignificant in comparison with the achievement of his most recent collection, *The Fire Next Time,* which consisted of a short "Letter to My Nephew on the One Hundredth Anniversary of the Emancipation" and a long essay, "Down at the Cross" (published first in the *New Yorker* magazine in November 1962), on, among other things, his own past, America's future, and a religious movement oftentimes referred to as the Black Muslims but known officially as the Nation of Islam.

The Fire Next Time brought Baldwin an inordinate amount of acclaim. While its author was being featured on the cover of national magazines, appearing regularly on television and radio, and serving as the subject of numerous newspaper articles, the book shot to the very top of the nonfiction best-seller lists and remained in the top five for 41 weeks. With his success and fame, Baldwin chose to devote an increasing amount of his time and energy to the civil rights movement, using his skills as a writer to report from the front lines, where black students were menaced by white mobs as they tried to integrate formerly all-white educational facilities and black churches were bombed while little children attended Sunday school, and his high profile as a celebrated author as a pulpit from which to articulate the aspirations and goals of the movement. The writer befriended most of the leaders of the movement, who were quick to recognize the importance he could have for them as a symbol and, more important, as a spokesman.

Though critics would charge that Baldwin's political engagement came at the expense of his literary art, his resounding, fiery oratory, in which was combined his keen intellect, precise yet poetic language, and the rhetorical skills and moral conviction of his past as a child minister in New York City—"he impressed me as resembling an Old Testament prophet," one observer later recalled—was soon being heard at innumerable rallies, fundraisers, and demonstrations. Increasingly, this commitment to political causes left Baldwin with little time and energy to spare for his writing, but he persisted, preaching a compassionate message of love for the architects and defenders of white supremacy—"we cannot be free until they are free," he wrote—seeking to answer for himself and his listeners the question he had posed for the Nation of Islam's leader, Elijah Muhammad, in "Down at the Cross": "Isn't love more important than color?"

It was a question that, despite numerous setbacks, discouragements, and heartbreaks, Baldwin sought always to convince his audience must be answered affirmatively. It is only "love that takes off the masks that we fear that we cannot live without and know we cannot live within," is the way the author put it in "Down at the Cross," which is why it is both "so desperately sought and so cunningly avoided." Only by shedding these masks, Baldwin believed—the illusions and untruths that, in the United States, whites and blacks hold about one another, and that all individuals hold about others, and that we hold about ourselves—can we grow, as a nation and as individuals.

"The relationship one is trying to establish," Baldwin would tell an interviewer in 1965 in response to a question as to what kind of relationship between whites and blacks in the United States he was hoping for, "hopefully, at least among a few people, as a model and a possibility and as an example for the rest, is simply a human one. Because color simply does not matter, and it doesn't have to be the affliction which it is in so many of our lives for all our lives. There are ways to break the nightmare if one is willing to deal with one's self and tell the truth to one's self."

So Baldwin accepted Forman's invitation and the media came to Selma as well and Baldwin feared for his life. He had grown up in the urban North, in Harlem in New York City, and had for much of the last 15 years lived as an expatriate in Paris, France; he had not even made his first visit to the South until 1957, when word of the early battles in the civil rights movement brought him back from overseas.

In the South, Baldwin felt both at home and in danger. "Negroes in the North are right when they refer to the South as the Old Country," he wrote in his essay "Nobody Knows My Name." "A Negro born in the North who finds himself in the South is in a position similar to that of the son of the Italian emigrant who finds himself in Italy, near the village where his father first saw the light of day. Both are in countries they have never seen, but which they cannot fail to recognize." Part of that recognition, for Baldwin and other blacks, was of the South's legacy of violent racial oppression.

"The South has always frightened me," Baldwin explained in the essay "A Fly in Buttermilk," which, like "Nobody Knows My Name," recounts his impressions of his first visits to that torn region. "How deeply it had frightened me—though I had never seen it—and how soon, was one of the things my dreams revealed to me while I was there." The images it evoked in him, born from the tales told him in his childhood by his southern-born parents, relatives, and neighbors, were of shootings and rapes and lynchings, of flaming crosses left in yards as the calling cards of white men hidden behind white sheets who rode by night. "I could not suppress the thought that this earth had acquired its color from the blood that dripped down from these trees," Baldwin, in "Nobody Knows My Name," records himself as thinking as he observes for the first time, from the window of his circling airplane, the red clay of Georgia. "My mind filled with the image of a black man, younger than I, perhaps, or my own age, hanging from a tree while white men watched him and cut his sex from him with a knife."

And by 1963, Baldwin recognized, southern whites had grown no less violent, no less ruthless, in seeking to defend their system of oppression, and the risks to those who would challenge the southern way of life were no less grave. For all his celebrity, on a line with 325 other African Americans in front of the Dallas County Courthouse in Selma, Baldwin was no different from them: a black man with the audacity to claim his constitutional rights. In fact, in the eyes of many white southerners, he was something even worse—one of the dreaded

"outside agitators" from the North come down to "stir up" the area's black population, who would otherwise, so such thinking went, be peacefully content with their lot.

The would-be voters were subjected to persistent harassment, of the kind the southern white policemen and government officials had by then perfected. The county sheriff and his deputies intimidated them

Baldwin explains the tactics and objectives of the civil rights movement at a church service in Paris in August 1963. The passion and fervor of his teenage years as a Pentecostal preacher were still evident in his oratory.

by threatening arrests for blocking the sidewalk. Those who left the line—to relieve themselves, for example—were not allowed to rejoin it. The police prevented friends and family from bringing food and drink to those who were lined up outside in the hot sun, while inside the courthouse, registration officials did everything in their power to make sure that the line moved as slowly as possible. When Baldwin attempted to speak with the people in line, he was threatened with arrest. When he and Forman went to the head of the line to find out why the process was taking so unusually long, they were told to go to the side door of the courthouse. When they went to the side door, they were told to go to the front door. At the end of the tension-ridden day, fewer than 50 people, according to the *New York Times,* had been registered to vote. Baldwin put the figure at closer to 20.

At several times during the frustrating day, friends worried that they might have to restrain Baldwin from a personal confrontation with the imposing Sheriff Clark. Emotional, even volatile, Baldwin, despite his small size—five-foot-six, approximately 135 pounds—never let his fears rule him, and by this time, he later wrote, his terror was being "swallowed up by rage." Indeed, he often impressed others as a tiny ball of fury, someone who kept himself contained only through tremendous force of will. "His head was formidable with big, incredibly expressive eyes and a wide mouth that frequently flashed gap-toothed grins," his biographer W. J. Weatherby wrote. "His slight, erect body . . . was like a frail wire connected to a big bulb that continually lit up. You noticed only the intense look of his dark face and especially the eyes, which were peacefully friendly . . . but which I was to see flash like fire when he was passionately involved in an argument." Baldwin described himself as "a very tight, tense, lean, abnormally intelligent and hungry black cat."

Fearful of the rage that boiled up within him outside the Dallas County courthouse, Baldwin eventually retired to the SNCC headquarters with a bottle of whiskey—his common self-prescription for a body and soul subjected to so much physical and psychic stress—to repair his frayed nerves. "I saw him fluctuating between hope and despair," a friend, the eminent psychologist and educator Kenneth B.

Clark, said about Baldwin during this time. "He was concerned about the future of America. He saw a lack of concern or an inability in this nation to deal ethically with the problems of race."

Yet despite his very real fear and frustration and anger, James Baldwin remained in Selma for days, conquering his inner demons and standing up to the hatemongers, speaking to reporters, into the camera, lending support to his fellow African Americans. In the tumultuous battle with others and with himself that marked his long, brilliant career, it was this single element, more than any other, that allowed him to succeed: courage—moral courage, physical courage, artistic courage, personal courage. Regardless of the multitude of obstacles in his life—being black, gay, poor—he somehow found the fortitude to write and speak the truth as he saw it, no matter how painful, controversial, or dangerous. Repeatedly, he spoke and wrote of the importance of *seeing* as a means to the truth: "I suspect, though I certainly cannot prove it, that every life moves full circle—towards revelation: You begin to see, and even rejoice to see, what you always saw. . . . It's a difficult relationship, but mysteriously indispensable. It teaches you." No lesson comes for free, Baldwin often tells us in his work, and he asks often if we are willing to pay "the price of the ticket," as he would name, near the end of his life and career, the single-volume collection of his essays. The price? Courage. A price he paid again and again.

PEACE ON EARTH

James A. Baldwin

Illustrated by John Baldwin

I

T was a dreary snowy day in December. It was the kind of day that makes a fellow wish he had never been born. The sky was overcast and ominous. as far as the eye could see, the earth was covered with a heavy white blanket.

The day was still and quiet, and to us in the dugout it was oppressive. It made us think of peace, of homes, of Christmas chimes ringing through the air. And when one is at the front fighting for one's country, it is no time to be thinking of home.

I looked about me. There were four of us in the dugout. Stan, Pete, and I, Scotty, were three negro boys. Johnny, the youngest and most religious of us, was white. We were four pals. We had gone to school together. We came from the same town, and loved each other. We loved peace. The only reason we were fighting was that we had been drafted. We had not chosen to murder human beings whom we had never seen before.

I looked at Stan. He was the largest of us all. He was writing a let- ter to the

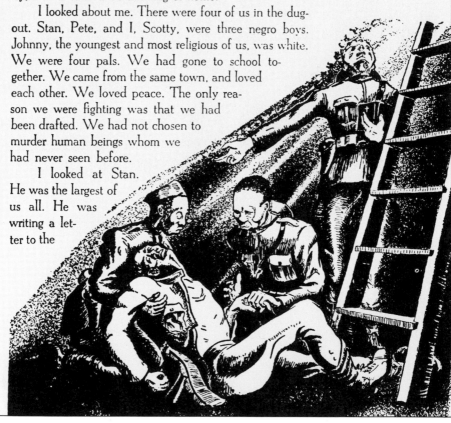

CHAPTER TWO

IN MY FATHER'S HOUSE

The title page of one of the stories Baldwin wrote for the *Magpie,* the student literary magazine at De Witt Clinton High School in the Bronx. "It was perfectly apparent that he was an extraordinary kid," a high school classmate, Emile Capouya, later recalled.

James Arthur Baldwin was born on August 2, 1924, at Harlem Hospital in New York City, to Emma Berdis Jones and an unknown father. Though he would not discover—apparently by accident, by way of an overheard conversation—that he had been born illegitimate until he was a teenager, the revelation that he did not know the identity of his biological father would haunt him for the rest of his life, for his mother simply refused to answer his questions on the subject. As Weatherby points out, the title of Baldwin's second collection of essays, *Nobody Knows My Name,* would always have an "ironic double meaning for him," referring not just to a social and political climate in which whites, as Baldwin believed, knew nothing of the true identity of blacks (whose ancestors had had their names stolen from them in slavery) but also to the mystery surrounding his own ancestry.

25

His mother had emigrated from Deals Island, Maryland, to New York City just after World War I. Though she was a tender and loving woman, he pointed out that his "mother's strength was only to be called on in a desperate emergency," for she had all she could do to feed, clothe, and raise a family of what would eventually be nine children while also working as a cleaning and laundry woman. One of Baldwin's grade-school teachers would later trace the origins of his literary talent to his mother; Berdis Baldwin had, the educator said, "the gift of using language beautifully." As a child, Baldwin would sometimes feel that his mother was too gentle and forgiving, but in later life he would cite her strength as her most important character trait, and he gave her much credit for recognizing and respecting the individuality of each of her children. "You have lots of brothers and sisters," he remembered her saying to them. "You don't know what's going to happen to them. So you're to treat everybody like your brothers and sisters. Love them."

"I was the only child in the house—or houses—for a while," Baldwin would later write in his memoir *No Name in the Street,* "a halcyon period which memory has quite repudiated; and if I remember myself as tugging at my mother's skirts and staring up into her face, it was because I was so terrified of the man we called my father."

Baldwin's "father" was the man his mother married when James was three: David Baldwin, a laborer and Pentecostal preacher who had been born in Bunkie, Louisiana, sometime near the end of the Civil War and came to New York in 1919 as part of a great wave of post–World War I northward emigration by African Americans seeking better social conditions and economic opportunities. "No one," Baldwin wrote in the essay "Notes of a Native Son," "including my father, seems to have known exactly how old he was, but his mother had been born in slavery." The mother, Barbara Baldwin, lived with her son's family in Harlem until her death in 1930; it was from her that young James first heard stories of life under slavery and in the post-emancipation South. Though he and his father (as James always referred to David Baldwin) talked much less often—"when he was dead I realized that I had hardly ever spoken to him"—James gathered that life in the South had been no less painful for him. "They were hanging niggers from trees in uniforms in 1919 and my father left the South therefore," James would later say.

In New York, David Baldwin remarried, found work at a bottle factory on Long Island, and began to preach in storefront churches throughout Harlem on Sundays and on certain nights of the week, but the frustrations that had driven him from the South would, in a relatively short time, overwhelm him in the North.

Together, David and Berdis Baldwin would have eight children: three boys—George, Wilmer, and David—and five girls—Barbara, Gloria, Ruth, Elizabeth, and Paula Maria. In addition, one of David Baldwin's sons from a previous marriage, Samuel, lived with the family, until his father's unrelieved bitterness and anger drove him away permanently in 1932.

Though David Baldwin worked steadily, until encroaching age and illness prohibited it, his wages were never enough to feed his large family, particularly once, beginning in 1929, the American economy was devastated by the Great Depression and he was sometimes laid off from his job. With rent money often difficult to come by, the family was forced to move frequently, to various apartments, all of them in Harlem between the Harlem River and Lenox Avenue on the east and west and 135th and 131st streets on the north and south. In later years, Baldwin often said that he grew up feeling that he had never had enough to eat; at times, the Baldwins subsisted on relief donations of canned corned beef and stewed prunes, and at Thanksgiving, James and his brother George lined up in the street outside the Cotton Club, Harlem's entertainment showcase, for free turkey dinners. In "Notes of a Native Son," Baldwin would "wonder what it could have felt like for such a man to have nine children whom he could barely feed" and how much this situation had contributed to his father's "intolerable bitterness of spirit."

For whatever reasons, David Baldwin was a brutally severe man. In "Notes of a Native Son," one of Baldwin's most moving works, he traces the process of understanding whereby he came to a sort of posthumous reconciliation with his father's memory. "He was not a young man when we were growing up," Baldwin wrote, "and he had already suffered many kinds of ruin; in his outrageously demanding and protective way he loved his children who were black like him and menaced like him; and all these things sometimes showed in his face when he tried, never to my knowledge with any success, to establish contact with us." Indeed, on those rare occasions when he tried to play with one of his children or help them with their homework, they would become paralyzed with fright and he would become angry. "I do not remember, in all those years, that one of his children was ever glad to see him come home," wrote Baldwin.

If, as Baldwin wrote, his father was sometimes capable of "a rather crushing charm," his family saw more often his anger. "It had something to do with his blackness," Baldwin would speculate in "Notes of a Native Son," "with his blackness and his beauty and the fact that he knew he was black but did not know he was beautiful. He claimed to be proud of his blackness, but it had to have been the cause of much humiliation and it fixed bleak boundaries to his life." On the pulpit, that anger was directed in words at the "white devils" whom David Baldwin so passionately hated, but it was acted out against his family. "Indescribably cruel in his personal life," David Baldwin beat any and all of the children on the slightest pretext, but James—perhaps because of his illegitimacy, he would come to feel—was the special target of his wrath. In addition to administering frequent beatings, his father repeatedly told James that he was the ugliest child he had ever seen, and he cruelly nicknamed the boy Frog Eyes. On one occasion, in the dead of an extremely cold winter, his father gave James his last dime to buy kerosene from the local store. Little Jimmy slipped on the ice and fell, losing the money; when his father found out, he beat him with the cord to an electric iron until the boy passed out. Over and over again, his father pointed out that as a black boy he could expect nothing but hatred and misery from the world. "He frightened me so much that no man has ever frightened me since," Baldwin later remembered, and many nights he cried himself to sleep.

Remarkably, James Baldwin would one day find the courage to refrain from despising his father, a process he eloquently charts in "Notes of a Native Son." Whereas many would have harbored an awful hurt for the rest of their lives, Baldwin struggled to understand. "He formed me," he told an interviewer near the end of his own life, "and he raised me, and he did not let me starve. . . . He claimed me as a son. He gave me myself. I may not always like that self . . . yet here it is, and here I am, and I would not be here had it not been for him."

As the oldest child, much of the responsibility for caring for his younger brothers and sisters fell on James. "He was my right arm," his mother later said. "He took care of them all. . . . He'd get them to bed and then say, 'Is there anything else I could do for you, Mama?'" An insatiable reader from an early age, young Jimmy, when he was not in school, could usually be found in his family's overcrowded apartment, a baby in one arm, a book in his other hand. "I read books like they were some weird kind of food," he later told Weatherby.

For his father, young James's intellectual curiosity was just another source of danger. According to David Baldwin, the Bible was the only book worth reading. Indeed, as far as Baldwin's stepfather was concerned, "bright black boys with ambition . . . could be a menace to themselves and to those around them," James Campbell, a Baldwin biographer, would write. But for James, books provided him with a world outside of the poverty and struggles he knew and provided him with the insight that he was not the only one who had endured such hardship, and he had no intention of giving them up. "You read something which you thought only happened to you," Baldwin told journalist Studs Terkel in an interview in 1961, "and you discover it happened 100 years ago to Dostoyevsky. This is a very great liberation for the suffering, struggling person, who always thinks that he is alone."

Before he even entered high school, Baldwin was reading novels by the English writer Charles Dickens and the Russian author Feodor Dostoyevsky, but his favorite novel was *Uncle Tom's Cabin,* by the American abolitionist Harriet Beecher Stowe. Set on a plantation in the antebellum South, the novel delineates the myriad horrors of life under slavery. First published in 1852, the novel was so influential in crystallizing abolitionist sentiment that Abraham Lincoln is supposed to have asked, upon being introduced to its author, "Is this the little woman whose book made such a great war [the Civil War]?" and the names of two of its most important characters—Uncle Tom, the eternally loyal and pious slave, and Simon Legree, his brutal owner—have become a permanent part of the American language.

In later years, Baldwin recalled that he "had read *Uncle Tom's Cabin* compulsively, the book in one hand, the newest baby on my hipbone. I was trying to find out something, sensing something in the book of some immense import to me: which, however, I knew I did not really understand." Sensing something amiss in her son's obsession with the novel, Berdis Baldwin hid it from him. "The last time she hid it, she

Vegetable stands on the corner of Fifth Avenue and 135th Street in Harlem in the late 1920s. Though predominantly African American even then, Harlem was a much more racially diverse neighborhood in Baldwin's youth than it is today, and a strong sense of community prevailed. As an adult, Baldwin remembered that if he misbehaved in public, one of his neighbors was sure to "whip my behind and carry me, howling, to my house."

hid it on the highest shelf above the bathtub. I was somewhere around seven or eight." He found the book anyway, and after that his mother "didn't hide it anymore, and indeed, from that moment, though in fear and trembling, began to let me go."

Although Baldwin could be a shy, even sullen, child, his intellectual precocity was immediately apparent to his teachers. Small and frail, somewhat effeminate in manner even when very young, he was often picked on at school by the other children, who teased him about his appearance and his ragged clothes. He responded by withdrawing, but several educators recognized that the unsmiling boy was someone special, and in a short time Baldwin learned that quick wits and intelligence could be used to win approval.

At Baldwin's first school, P.S. 24, a remarkable woman named Gertrude Ayer, who was the first and at that time the only black principal in the New York City school system, took a special interest in him. "She liked me," Baldwin told Kenneth Clark in an interview in 1963. "In a way I guess she proved to me that I didn't have to be entirely defined by my circumstances." With her encouragement, he began to write stories, plays, and poems, some of them penned on grocery bags when his family could not spare money for him to buy paper. Another dedicated educator, Orilla "Bill" Miller, a white woman from the Midwest, overcame David Baldwin's objections—the theater, movies, and secular music were strictly forbidden in the Baldwin household, and education was suspect as a tool of the white devils not particularly useful to black men in a racist society that placed so many checks on their ambition—and regularly took Jimmy downtown to plays and films. Later, when David Baldwin began to have a hard time holding on to work, she helped the family survive a particularly difficult winter with donations of food and other necessities. "It is certainly partly because of her," Weatherby quotes Baldwin as saying in later life, "that I never really managed to hate white people."

At Frederick Douglass Junior High School, Baldwin continued his literary efforts, contributing short stories, editorials, and sketches to the school magazine, *The Douglass Pilot,* and receiving encouragement from a French instructor at the school, Countee Cullen, a celebrated poet of the Harlem Renaissance. Another teacher, Herman Porter, introduced Baldwin to the magnificent New York Public Library on 42nd Street, where he did research on an article he was writing for the school magazine on the history of Harlem. The trip, apparently taken over his father's objections, made Baldwin so nervous that he vomited, but he returned again and again, even after, during one downtown visit, he overhead a policeman mutter, "Why can't you niggers stay uptown where you belong?" as he passed by.

Around the age of 14, in the summer before he began attending prestigious De Witt Clinton High School in the Bronx, Baldwin underwent what he described as a "prolonged religious crisis." He had been raised, of course, in a household atmosphere of strict, even suffocating, religiosity. "I was born in the church," he would write in the introduction to his play *The Amen Corner*; his father, he wrote in "Notes of a Native Son," lived "like a prophet, in such unimaginably close communion with the Lord that his long silences which were punctuated by moans and hallelujahs and snatches of old songs while he sat at the living room window never seemed strange to us."

Moreover, the community he lived in was dotted with churches, from the famous Abyssinian Baptist Church to the numerous storefront houses of worship where his father preached and the members of various Pentecostal sects—Holy Rollers, they were often called—waited to be visited by the Holy Spirit, and which he would describe so evocatively in his first novel, *Go Tell It on the Mountain*. For the transplanted southerners who made up the majority of Harlem's black population, the church was the most tangible connection to their American roots, the most palpable legacy of their southern past. "I was born into a Southern community displaced into the streets of New York," Campbell quotes Baldwin as telling a class of university students in 1984. "And what did we bring with us? What did my father bring with him? He brought with him his Bible. He, and others like him, with their Bibles and their hymn books, managed to rent a space which had been a store and took out the fixtures, built a pulpit, got a piano, a tambourine—and it became a church."

Baldwin had attended the raucous, celebratory, music-filled services at such churches ever since he was a very young boy, but he had, with all the immense willpower he had begun to forge out of his daunting circumstances and the terrible, never-ending quarrel with his father— "knowing his life and his pain taught me how to fight," he told an interviewer in 1976—resisted religion's call on his soul. Countless times he had sat among the faithful, "the saints," as he described in *Go Tell It on the Mountain,* as they "sang with all the strength that was in them, and clapped their hands for joy," but "there had never been a time when [he] had not sat watching the saints rejoice with terror in his heart, and wonder. Their singing caused him to believe in the presence of the Lord; indeed, it was no longer a question of belief, because they made that presence real. He did not feel it himself, the joy they felt, yet he could not doubt that it was, for them, the very bread of life—could not doubt it, that is, until it was too late to doubt."

"Everyone had always said that John would be a preacher when he grew up, just like his father. It had been said so often that John, without ever thinking about it, had come to believe it himself." John is John Grimes, the 14-year-old protagonist of *Go Tell It on the Mountain,* and the passage quoted is the first two sentences of the novel. Though it is always risky to read fiction as biography, Baldwin's first novel is clearly autobiographical, and it provides some insight into the forces that provoked his spiritual crisis in his 14th year. Young John, the oldest boy in a large, impoverished Harlem family, an extremely intelligent, illegitimate, undersized, lonely child, who dreams of being "beautiful, tall and popular" but is teased as Frog Eyes by other children, is locked in conflict with a bitter, brutal, God-obsessed father, who is a preacher; in the duration of a long night in a storefront church, the Temple of the Fire Baptized, much of it spent writhing and rolling on the "threshing-floor" in the possession of the Holy Spirit, he is "saved." In the course of the novel, the reader also learns of the pasts of the three most important adults in John's life—his mother, his father, and his father's sister—and Baldwin provides a fictional answer to the mystery of the true identity of his biological father.

Similar conflicts in Baldwin's own life led him to the security of religious belief. As he reached adolescence, the menaces and terrors that his father had so often evoked in his sermons and tirades suddenly became real for him. "What I saw around me that summer in Harlem," Baldwin wrote in "Down at the Cross," "was what I had always seen; nothing had changed. But now, without any warning, the whores and pimps and racketeers on the avenue had become a personal menace. It had not before occurred to me that I could become one of them, but now I realized that we had been produced by the same circumstances." And the closer he looked at the world around him, the fewer options he saw for himself. Even his intelligence and education (should he be lucky enough to complete it) would not be enough to protect him from the world of the ghetto that now seemed to threaten to swallow him up: "School began to reveal itself, therefore, as a child's game that one could not win, and boys dropped out of school and went to work. My father wanted me to do the same. I refused, even though I no longer had any illusions about what an education could do for me; I had already encountered too many college-graduate handymen. . . . One did not have to be very bright to realize how little one could do to change one's situation."

Much of the fear and confusion that now tormented him was connected with his adolescent discovery of his sexuality. His friends, Baldwin wrote, had begun "to drink and smoke, and embarked—at first avid, and then groaning—on their sexual careers." The birth of sexual desire made him, he wrote in "Down at the Cross," "afraid of the evil within me. . . . Owing to the way I had been raised, the abrupt discomfort that all this aroused in me and the fact that I had no idea what my voice or my mind or my body was likely to do next caused me to consider myself one of the most depraved people on earth." Though, Baldwin wrote, he would surrender "to a spiritual seduction long before I came to any carnal knowledge . . . everything inflamed me, and that was bad enough."

This confusion and fear was worsened by his growing realization that, unlike the majority of his peers, he was more attracted sexually to males than he was to females. "All art is a kind of confession," Baldwin would later say on several occasions; in *Go Tell It on the Mountain,* young John Grimes is tormented by the notion of his own sinfulness, not just in the form of his emerging sexuality but the direction it takes: "He had sinned. In spite of the saints, his mother and his father, the warnings he had heard from his earliest beginnings, he had sinned with his hands a sin that was hard to forgive. In the school lavatory, alone, thinking of the boys, older, braver, bigger, who made bets with each other as to whose urine could arch higher, he had watched in himself a transformation of which he would never dare to speak."

So Baldwin sought shelter—from himself and from the world outside—in the church. "I then discovered God, His saints and angels, and His blazing Hell," he wrote in "Down at the Cross." "I supposed Him to exist only within the walls of a church—in fact, of *our* church—and I also supposed that God and safety were synonymous." A friend took him to the Mount Calvary of the Pentecostal Faith Church on Lenox Avenue, where he met its charismatic priestess, the famous Mother Horn. One night, after listening to her preach, he had an experience very like that undergone by John Grimes near the conclusion of *Go Tell It on the Mountain.* "I became more guilty and more frightened, and kept all this bottled up inside me," he wrote in "Down at the Cross," "and naturally, inescapably, one night, when this woman had finished preaching, everything came roaring, screaming, crying out, and I fell to the ground before the altar. It was the strangest sensation I have ever had in my life. . . . One moment I was on my feet . . . the next moment, with no transition, no sensation of falling, I was on my back, with the lights beating down into my face and all the vertical saints above me. I did not know what I was doing down so low, or how I had got there. And the anguish that filled me cannot be described." He spent the entire night on the "threshing-floor," while around him the saints "sang and rejoiced and prayed. And in the morning, when they raised me, they told me that I was 'saved.'"

At age 14, "realiz[ing] immediately that I could not remain in the church merely as another worshiper," Baldwin became a young minister at the Fireside Pentecostal Assembly. Relying on his knowledge of the Bible and on divine inspiration—the spirit speaking directly to the congregation through the instrument of the minister—rather than on a written text, he preached every Sunday and sometimes during the week for the next three years, noting with satisfaction that his popularity as a preacher quickly outstripped his father's. "Nothing that has happened to me since," Baldwin wrote in "Down at the Cross," "equals the power and the glory that I sometimes felt when, in the middle of a sermon, I knew that I was somehow, by some miracle, really carrying, as they said, 'the Word'—when the church and I were one." Later, the talent for extemporaneous oratory that he developed as a preacher would help him earn a reputation as a riveting public speaker. "I've never written a speech," he told interviewers from the *Paris Review* in 1984. "I can't *read* a speech. It's kind of give and take. You have to sense the people you're talking to. You have to respond to what they hear."

There is little doubt that James Baldwin was the most unusual student at De Witt Clinton High School. His color, for one, made him stand out; there were few blacks at Clinton, the student body of which consisted mainly of the children of European immigrants, many of whom were Jewish. Baldwin is also remembered as the poorest student in his class and certainly as the only one who was a preacher. "He was still very holy in those days," a classmate later recalled.

The new friends he made also recognized rather quickly that Baldwin's sexual orientation set him apart. Though Baldwin talked about girls, "I assumed from day one of knowing him that Jimmy's preferences were gay," said the future editor and publisher Sol Stein. An even closer friend from high school, Emile Capouya, also remembered that Baldwin sometimes expressed interest in girls and still "hadn't made up his mind about his homosexual nature," but it seems likely that this interest was less genuine than an attempt to ease his guilt and confusion by channeling or masking his sexuality in a more socially acceptable form, for to one even closer to Baldwin than Capouya, there was never any doubt about Baldwin's sexuality. "Honey, I knew when Jimmy was a little boy. Of course we just knew," David Baldwin, James's youngest brother, replied in later life when asked when the family first realized that Baldwin was gay.

RODERICK G. ARMSTRONG
"Rod"   C.C.N.Y.
Program Comm.; Service L.
Archaeologist
They always said I'd be a ditch
digger.

RICHARD P. AVONDA
"Richie"   C.C.N.Y.
Physics Sq.; Italian Club; Newman
Club; Lib. Sq.
Mechanical Engineer
About time!!

MILTON J. ARONDS
"Moogy"   Rochester
Program Sq.
To know all the answers
Do unto others before they do
unto you.

JOSEPH D. AZZNARA
"Azzi"   Fordham
Service L.; Locker Sq.
Science Teacher
To be or not to be this June, that
is the question.

RUSSELL HAMILTON ARONDS
"Russ"   Rutgers
Locker Sq.; Service L.; Lunchroom
Sq.; Biology Sq.; Lib. Sq.
Salesman
"I cash clothes."

JAMES A. BALDWIN
"Baldy"   C.C.N.Y.
Magpie Editorial Board; Student
Court.
Novelist-Playwright
Fame is the spur and—ouch!

ALAN B. ARONSOHN
"Al"   Dartmouth
Regents Book Sq.; Admit and Pro-
gram Comm.
To fly to Hawaii
What did Howard Hughes ever
do to deserve all that?

JOHN F. BAME
"Jack"   Texas Christian
Engineer
I came, I slept, I graduated.

MORTON ASCH
"Morty"   C.C.N.Y.
Clintonian; Service L.
Writer
Clinton's gift to the intellectual
world.

ROBERT R. BANKS
"Bob"   Columbia
Arista; Pres., Sec. Sq. C; Pres.,
Sec. Chem. Club; Chem. Sq.;
Physics Sq.; Analytical Chem. Sq.
Chemist
No knock—I use Ethyl.

Part of the first page of the *Clintonian,*
the De Witt Clinton yearbook, from
Baldwin's senior year. Baldwin is in the
righthand column, third from top. As
his yearbook entry indicates, Baldwin's
ambition was already well defined: to
become a novelist and playwright and
achieve fame.

But the most important characteristic that set Baldwin apart, even at so academically distinguished an institution as Clinton, was his intellectual prowess. Though, for various reasons, he did not always receive exceptional grades—he had always been and continued to be abysmal at math, his father sometimes forbade him to study, and the demands of preaching sometimes kept him away from his homework, as did the necessity of taking part-time work in order to help his family financially—students and teachers alike recognized his exceptional intelligence. He was "an obvious genius," Capouya said. Stein cited his "ferocious involvement with language." Several teachers noted his modesty along with his already evident literary talent; one called him an "intellectual giant." Baldwin served on the staff of the school's ambitious literary magazine, *The Magpie,* and contributed stories, poems, plays, and even an interview with his former teacher Countee Cullen; in his senior year, he served as the magazine's editor.

The brilliant young student was now grappling with several opposing forces. The narrow world of his father, with his harsh religion and his suspicion of all things associated with white people, stood in opposition to the son's ever-expanding intellectual horizons, stimulated in large part by white teachers and his friendship with white students; the adolescent's developing sexuality, particularly in its orientation, was at odds with the self-denial preached by the fiery young minister. (And by his own recollection and that of his friends, Baldwin was an extraordinary preacher.) Although for most individuals, adolescence is a time of contradiction and struggle to form and to understand one's identity, it seems likely that Baldwin's struggle was more difficult than most. To further complicate matters, it was at around the age of 16, according to Weatherby, that Baldwin discovered the secret of his illegitimacy. Emile Capouya remembered discussing Baldwin's discovery with him at that time, and that his friend was "very emotional, very tearful about it."

Friends saw signs of the conflict within Baldwin. In the *Magpie* offices, Baldwin would sometimes give mock sermons, Capouya recalled, complete with tambourine playing and a "trance." At the same time, however, Capouya remembers him being torn by guilt whenever

For Baldwin, the painter Beauford Delaney (pictured) was "the first walking, living proof for me that a black man could be an artist." Baldwin later said of Delaney, "Following him around, watching him work, taught me something. Without him an already rocky road would have been much rockier."

he attended a movie—one of the many pleasures forbidden by his father and his religion. Baldwin also often spoke to Capouya about his sexual confusion.

According to Baldwin, it was Capouya who provided him with an introduction to a man who would prove to be one of the single greatest influences on his life, one who would help convince him to trust his artistic sensibilities. Beauford Delaney was 39 years old when the 16-year-old Baldwin first climbed the stairs to his studio on Greene Street in Greenwich Village in 1940 and was already a well-respected painter who would win considerable fame for his portraits of such important African Americans as W. E. B. Du Bois and W. C. Handy.

"I was terrified," Baldwin later wrote, "once I had climbed those stairs and knocked on the door. A short, round brown man came to the door and looked at me. He had the most extraordinary eyes I'd ever seen. . . . He smiled and said, 'Come in,' and opened the door." What followed was a teacher-student relationship and friendship that would endure until Delaney's death in 1979. So far as his artistic awakening was concerned, Baldwin told an interviewer in 1976, Delaney "was the most important person in my life." It was Delaney who introduced Baldwin to the music—forbidden in his home—of such blues greats as Bessie Smith and Ma Rainey and the incomparable jazz singer Billie Holiday. For the first time, Baldwin heard the jazz trumpet of Louis Armstrong, and Delaney took him to see and hear the magnificent black

American contralto Marian Anderson. To Baldwin, whose musical exposure had been limited to gospel songs and spirituals, the music of these innovators came as a revelation that taught him a new way of hearing and understanding the world, and blues, gospel music, and jazz would exert a profound influence on his work, offering him, in a way that literature did not, the possibility of working in a distinctly African American cultural tradition. "When I realized that music rather than American literature was really my language," Baldwin said in 1976, "I was no longer afraid. And then I could really write."

Perhaps most important, according to Baldwin, Delaney showed him how to *see*, to see as a painter sees, and as a writer must see: clearly. He remembered this most valuable of Delaney's lessons in a 1984 interview with the editors of the *Paris Review*. Baldwin and Delaney were standing on a street corner in Greenwich Village, waiting for the light to change, when the painter "pointed down and said 'Look.' I looked and all I saw was water. And he said, 'Look again,' which I did, and I saw oil on the water and the city reflected in the puddle. It was a great revelation to me. I can't explain it. He taught me how to see, and how to trust what I saw. Painters have often taught writers how to see. And once you've had that experience you see differently."

Delaney was gay, but it is uncertain whether his relationship with Baldwin was sexual. Capouya, for one, thought not; though by Baldwin's own testimony—in "Here Be Dragons," an essay published in 1985—he engaged in his first love affair at around this time, it was not with the painter but with a handsome, black-haired Harlem racketeer of Spanish and Irish descent. Though the romance was short-lived— broken off by Baldwin for fear that gossip about his activities would reach his family—in later years he would remember the relationship as an important one, for the notion that an older man of some worldliness would find little Frog Eyes worthy of love came as a profound revelation to the boy. Baldwin recalled the love affair as a tender and beautiful experience—"I will be grateful to that man until the day I die"—and his lover as unusually kind. "I showed him all my poetry," he wrote in "Here Be Dragons," "because I had no one else in Harlem to show it to, and even now, I sometimes wonder what on earth his friends could have been thinking, confronted with stingy-brimmed, mustachioed, razor-toting Poppa and skinny, popeyed Me when he walked me (rarely) into various shady joints, I drinking ginger ale, he drinking brandy."

By this time, Baldwin was coming to recognize that the conflict within him—between art and religion, between his sexuality and the church, between what he was and what others would have him be—was irreconcilable. Others also saw as much. Capouya said that Baldwin at this point "was in the church but not of it," meaning that he no longer truly believed but for various reasons—he spoke of the "social impossibility" of a full-scale break—had not yet been able to officially leave. Taking note of the decreasing frequency of his sermons and attendance at services (and perhaps as well the gossip about his social life), the saints at the Fireside Pentecostal Assembly began to wonder if their young preacher was "cooling off." Even Baldwin's father, who was sinking slowly into insanity, recognized that his son was close to making a decision. "You'd rather write than preach, wouldn't you?" he astonished the boy (who answered yes) by one day asking; it was, according to Baldwin in "Notes of a Native Son," the "one time in all our life together when we had really spoken to one another."

He had come to conclude, Baldwin wrote in "Down at the Cross," that the church "was a mask for self-hatred and despair. The transfiguring power of the Holy Ghost ended when the service ended, and salvation stopped at the church door." The love the church taught only applied to those who belonged to the church; "when we were told to love everybody," he wrote, "I had thought that that meant *everybody*. But no, it applied only to those who believed as we did, and it did not apply to white people at all. . . . What was the point, the purpose, of *my* salvation if it did not permit me to behave with love toward others, no matter how they behaved toward me?" So one morning in 1941, he preached a final sermon and left the pulpit to meet Capouya at the movies. "I had made the break," he later told Weatherby, "but there were some things I couldn't ever give up. They're in my blood, you know. I've lived with them all my life."

CHAPTER THREE

I NO LONGER
KNEW WHO
I REALLY WAS

An overturned automobile burns on Lenox Avenue during the riots that erupted in Harlem in August 1943. "To smash something is the ghetto's chronic need," Baldwin wrote in his magnificent essay "Notes of a Native Son." "Most of the time it is the members of the ghetto who smash each other, and themselves."

Having left the church, young James Baldwin had one more break to make—to remove himself from his father's house. He had hoped, after graduating from high school, to attend the City College of New York, a tuition-free institution with an excellent academic reputation, but his family's financial need made it necessary for him to get a job instead. Emile Capouya helped him find work in Belle Mead, New Jersey, laying railroad track for an army installation at $80 a week. Though the job paid well more than twice what Baldwin could have expected to earn in New York City (and almost exactly three times what his father was earning), Baldwin would recall his time in New Jersey for reasons other than the opportunity it gave him to help provide for his family, as he would relate in "Notes of a Native Son."

Baldwin was no stranger to racism—even as a little boy he had been roughed up by two cops, called "nigger," and abandoned in a vacant lot—but he was unprepared for the level of hostility he would be exposed to in New Jersey, which African Americans sometimes sarcastically referred to as New Georgia. Although not codified in the written law, as was the case in the South, in many parts of New Jersey southern-style segregation was practiced, and many of the people with whom Baldwin worked were from the South. "I knew about the South, of course," Baldwin wrote in "Notes of a Native Son," "and about how southerners treated Negroes and how they expected them to behave, but it had never entered my mind that anyone would look at me and expect *me* to behave that way. I learned in New Jersey that to be a Negro meant, precisely, that one was never looked at but was simply at the mercy of the reflexes the color of one's skin caused in other people. . . . I knew about jim crow but I had never experienced it."

When Baldwin responded by acting "the way I always acted," he told the anthropologist Margaret Mead for their joint project, *A Rap on Race,* in 1971, he "just couldn't believe what happened—the kind of fury that erupted." According to Baldwin, his persistent one-man attempts at integration—denied service in restaurants, diners, bars, and other public places, he simply returned again and again—quickly made him "notorious," both on and off the job. After a series of dismissals and reinstatements, he was fired, for reasons that are not entirely clear. Baldwin later told Weatherby that his ultimate sacking came after one long lunch too many, but in "Notes of a Native Son" he clearly intimated that it was related to his refusal to comply with New Jersey's racial codes. Capouya suggested yet another reason: the work was strenuously physical, and the slight Baldwin was not quite up to it. "He never learned how to use a pick or a shovel," Weatherby quotes Capouya as saying. "When he walked he trailed the shovel behind him like a pup on a leash. It was quite funny to see." The foreman apparently was less amused, and Baldwin was let go.

Whatever the reason for Baldwin's dismissal, the treatment he experienced in New Jersey because of the color of his skin had a profound effect on him. In "Notes of a Native Son," he recalled the time he spent in New Jersey as "the year during which . . . I first contracted some dread, chronic disease," which he described as a recurring "rage in the blood" that infects every black person at some time in their life—the rage that ultimately destroyed his father.

In Baldwin, this "fever" first manifested itself several days after his firing, when he and a white friend went to the movies together in Trenton. After the show, the two went into a diner for a bite to eat, only to hear, for Baldwin, a familiar refrain from the counterman: "We don't serve Negroes here." With a sarcastic comment on the name of the establishment—the American Diner—Baldwin left, but once on the street, which appeared to him to be teeming with white people, all of them moving in a direction opposite his own so that it seemed they were holding him back, he snapped. "I felt, like a physical sensation, a *click* at the nape of my neck as though some interior string connecting my head to my body had been cut." He walked, blindly, until coming "to an enormous, glittering, and fashionable restaurant in which I knew not even the intercession of the Virgin Mary would cause me to be served." He entered nonetheless, and sat down, and when, inevitably, the waitress fearfully and apologetically told him that Negroes were not served there, he picked up "an ordinary water-mug half full of water" and hurled it at her, shattering a mirror behind the bar. A mob gave chase, but with his friend's intercession Baldwin escaped. He left New Jersey with a stunning insight: that his life was threatened not just by the prejudice and hatred of others, but by the hatred such prejudice engendered in his own heart. "I could not get over two facts," he wrote in "Notes of a Native Son." "One was that I could have been murdered. But the other was that I had been ready to commit murder."

Baldwin was made newly aware of the consequences of "surrendering" to the "rage in his blood" upon returning to Harlem in June 1943: his father, under the weight of a lifetime of rage and fear and hatred and creeping paranoia, had finally gone irretrievably mad and, suffering from tuberculosis as well, had been institutionalized on Long Island. David Baldwin died on July 29, 1943, the same day that his youngest daughter, Paula Maria, was born; his funeral was held three days later, on August 2, his stepson's 19th birthday, and he was buried the morning after that, his hearse rolling through glass-strewn streets that testified to Harlem's collective infection. The nation was at war, and the community had long been on edge, for the most part over reports of mistreatment of black soldiers at the various army training camps in the Deep South. "Everybody felt a directionless, hopeless bitterness," Baldwin wrote in "Notes of a Native Son," "as well as that panic which can scarcely be suppressed when one knows that a human being one loves is in danger, and beyond reach. . . . Perhaps the best way to sum all this up is to say that the people I knew felt, mainly, a peculiar kind of relief when they knew that their boys were being shipped out of the South, to do battle overseas" against Germany or Japan. When, on the afternoon of David Baldwin's funeral, a rumor, erroneous in its particulars, circulated that a white policeman had shot a black soldier in the back and killed him in the course of an argument over a woman in the lobby of Harlem's Braddock Hotel, mobs attacked and looted the various white-owned businesses that dominated Harlem's economy.

In the year that he had spent in New Jersey, Baldwin would later write, he had discovered the secret that brought him, for the first time, to some understanding of his father: "I had discovered the weight of white people in the world." Previously, he would write, "I had inclined to be contemptuous of my father for the condition of his life, for the condition of our lives," but "when his life had ended I began to wonder about that life and also, in a new way, to be apprehensive about my own." As the family "drove my father to the graveyard through a wilderness of broken glass," for the first time Baldwin was able to sympathize with his father, "who had gone down under an impossible burden"—the impossibility of protecting his children from, and preparing them for, a world that would despise them because of the color of their skin. There were things that they shared; his father's bitterness, Baldwin now recognized, had become his own.

But for Baldwin, such insight would lead to a deeper, more important revelation, one that would become the cornerstone of his personal, artistic, and political message. One had to find a way to overcome the bitterness; not to do so was "folly," and the consequences for such failure destruction and death, as evidenced by the shattered mirror of the restaurant in New Jersey, the broken glass that crunched under the wheels of the hearse, and the "relief" of his younger siblings that their father "would not be coming home any more."

"It was necessary to hold on to the things that mattered," he wrote at the conclusion of "Notes of a Native Son." "The dead man mattered, the new life mattered; blackness and whiteness did not matter; to believe that they did was to acquiesce to one's own destruction. Hatred, which could destroy so much, never failed to destroy the man who hated and this was an immutable law." The difficult task one was required somehow to perform, and that Baldwin laid out for himself, was to accept "life as it is" and human beings as they are, which is to accept the existence of injustice—yet still fight against it "with all one's strength." Though he would never be free of the fever—"this fever has recurred in me, and does, and will until the day I die"—with his father's death, "it now had been laid to my charge," Baldwin wrote, "to keep my own heart free of hatred and despair."

But the literary voice that would so beautifully express the force of these revelations was still in the formation, to emerge only after several years of artistic and personal searching. With the encouragement of Beauford Delaney, Baldwin left his family's apartment in Harlem in favor of a rented room in Greenwich Village, which had long been a haven for writers, painters, musicians, actors, and various noncon- formists, including gay men and lesbians. After an unsettled period of odd jobs and relentless barhopping, Baldwin took a steady if unexciting position as a waiter at a West Indian restaurant, spending most of his off-hours reading—especially William Shakespeare, John Milton, and T. S. Eliot (a particular favorite at the time)—writing poetry, and grappling unsuccessfully with an attempt to write an autobiographical novel, then titled either *Crying Holy* or *In My Father's House,* that would deal with his experience in the church, his relationship with his father, and his family's history.

He was still grappling as well with his sexuality. Although he told Capouya that he had now come clearly to understand that he was gay, he continued to have relationships with women, including a rather significant affair with a former girlfriend of Capouya's, with whom he claimed to have been in love. Several other relationships with white women proved less satisfying, largely because Baldwin concluded that his attraction for them went no deeper than the color of his skin. At times, he contented himself with one-night affairs with men he picked up in the Village's handful of gay bars but soon concluded that he was "debas[ing]" himself; more satisfying were somewhat longer relationships, which he later described as "brief" but "intense," with a couple of male Village friends whose identities remain unknown. (According to Weatherby, one died of a drug overdose, and the other was an "Italian" who served as a model for a character in *Another Country* and exhibited a protective attitude toward Baldwin.) Though Baldwin was usually forthright in his literary and personal approach to homosexuality, the details of his personal life remain elusive; he was always, in print, sensitive to the privacy of his former lovers and almost never named names. Clearly, he was still working toward an understanding of his sexuality; Weatherby quotes him as saying "I was afraid that I already seemed and sounded too much like a woman," and he would continue to have relationships with members of both sexes for several years to come.

At the end of 1944, Baldwin made a friendship that would prove nearly as significant to his artistic development as his ongoing relationship with Delaney. Richard Wright was the most successful and well-known black writer in the world, arguably the most important black writer in the history of American literature. He had been born in 1908 in rural Mississippi to a poor sharecropper and his wife. He left home at 19 and worked his way north to Chicago, Illinois, where he eventually found work as a writer for the Chicago Writer's Project of the Works Progress Administration (WPA), one of several government agencies created during the Great Depression by the administration of Franklin D. Roosevelt to put the unemployed to work. In 1938, Wright's first book, a collection of four novellas entitled *Uncle Tom's Children,* garnered wide critical attention, but it was his novel *Native Son,* published in 1940, that earned Wright his reputation. The book is an unsparing portrayal of Bigger Thomas, a young black man living on the poverty-ridden South Side of Chicago, and of the social conditions that propel him to murder and the electric chair. The novel sold 250,000 copies in less than six weeks and became the first book by a black author to become a main selection of the Book-of-the-Month Club; more important, the novel brought the devastating effects of poverty and racism on African America to national attention, and it established Wright as a major literary voice. (According to the editors of the *Encyclopedia of Black America,* "the birth of the modern Afro-American novel is marked by the publication of Richard Wright's *Native Son* in 1940, in the same way that the modern English novel is dated by the 1740 edition of Samuel Richardson's *Pamela*.") To Baldwin, still struggling desperately with *Crying Holy,* Wright "was the greatest black writer in the world," as he later put it in his essay "Alas, Poor Richard." In Wright's work, he would write, "I found expressed, for the first time in my life, the sorrow, the rage, and the murderous bitterness which was eating up my life and the lives of those around me. His work was an immense liberation and revelation for me."

Wright was then living with his wife and daughter in Brooklyn and agreed, at the behest of a mutual friend, to meet Baldwin at his apartment. Gracious, somewhat shy, less imposing than Baldwin had expected, the famous novelist broke out a bottle of bourbon for his young guest and drew him out on the subject of his novel-in-progress. Eager to impress, Baldwin told him "far more about the novel than I, in fact, knew about it, madly improvising, one jump ahead of the bourbon, on all the themes which cluttered my mind." But Wright liked his young guest, surmised he had talent, and agreed to read the 60 or 70 pages of *Crying Holy* that Baldwin had completed. Baldwin mailed it to him the next day, and to his great delight—"He was so overcome with joy he could hardly speak," a Harper's editor recalled—Wright passed it on to his publishers, Harper & Brothers, who awarded Baldwin their Eugene F. Saxton Fellowship. Baldwin would receive $500; Harper took an option to publish the completed novel. He gave some of the money to his mother, for support of the family, and settled down to finish the novel.

For months Baldwin labored over the manuscript, working well into the night after his shift as a waiter was completed. By and by, he knew something was not quite right, that he had not yet found the language and the necessary elements of plot and characterization to pull together his novel as a seamless whole: to successfully tell his family's story. Nevertheless, he pressed on, uneasily, to complete the manuscript.

In confirmation of his worst fears, Harper declined the novel when it was presented, as, ultimately, did two other publishers. Baldwin was devastated and ashamed, too humiliated to face anyone, let alone Wright, whose confidence in him he felt he had betrayed. He went into hiding for a time, emerging only to immerse himself again in the Village social scene and for a brief meeting with Wright before the famous author, disheartened by racism and government harassment, relocated to Paris. He did not allow his discouragement to keep him down for long, however, and in a short time he mustered up the courage to try again. "My pride was massive in those days," he would later tell Weatherby. "It had to be to survive."

The front cover of *Go Tell It on the Mountain*, Baldwin's first novel, which has remained in print since its initial publication in 1953. The book is Baldwin's fictional exploration of his Harlem youth and of his family's southern roots.

Baldwin's hours in Village bars and restaurants were not strictly recreational, for he purposefully frequented those haunts where he was most likely to meet journalists and editors from whom he could obtain magazine assignments. Although his attempts to publish his novel had been stalled for the present, he soon was achieving some measure of success as a critic and contributor to some of the most important intellectual journals of the day—the *Nation, Commentary, Partisan Review,* and the *New Leader.* His first professional published work—a review of a collection of short stories by the Russian writer Maxsim Gorky—appeared in the April 12, 1947, issue of the *Nation.* After penning several book reviews for the *Nation* and the *New Leader,* including one in which he detected a homoerotic element in the relationship between the two main characters of Robert Louis Stevenson's classic novel, *Kidnapped,* Baldwin completed his first full-length essay, "Harlem Ghetto: Winter 1948," for the February 1948 issue of *Commentary.* The essay, which essentially concerned the difficult subject of black anti-semitism, was "a masterpiece," according to Baldwin's editor, Raymond Rosenthal. Ten months later, his first professional short story, "Previous Condition," appeared in the same journal.

For a writer so young, without a college education, to be published in such distinguished journals was no small accomplishment. Baldwin's editors—Philip Rahv, Elliott Cohen, Sol Levitas, Robert Warshow, and the esteemed poet Randall Jarrell—were among the foremost men of letters in the country, and they were unanimous in praising his insight, intelligence, and talent (if less enthusiastic about his habit of borrowing money). Still, his reviews, essays, and other short pieces brought him more acclaim than satisfaction, for he remained frustrated both professionally and personally. In later years, he would acknowledge the great debt he owed his editors (all of whom were white) from this time—"It is not too much to say that they helped to save my life," he would tell Weatherby—but he also came rather quickly to feel, according to later reminiscences, that he was in danger of being pigeonholed because of the color of his skin: that he was automatically assumed to be an expert on racial issues and generally assigned books and topics that dealt with racial matters.

Even more important, from a professional standpoint, were his continuing difficulties with *Crying Holy,* which he just could not shape to his satisfaction. Rahv recommended the novel to an editor at Random House, who deemed the manuscript still "not sufficiently strong, compelling, or even realized to carry the weight of the author's intentions." Another publishing project—a nonfiction text accompanying photographs of Harlem churches and dance halls taken by a friend named Theodore Pelatowski—won him $1,500 in the form of a Rosenwald Fellowship, but he and Pelatowski were unable to sell the book to a publisher.

His personal life was no less unsettled. He fell in love with a young black woman, Grace; the two lived together for a year, and Baldwin even bought her an engagement ring. He stopped short of actually asking her to marry him, however, recognizing that he was still attracted primarily to men; she had come into his life, he told Weatherby, "many light-years too late." It was at about this time that Baldwin began the practice of announcing his homosexuality to any new acquaintance, in the belief that if a person wanted nothing to do with him for that reason, he or she could make it known right then and there rather than later. If he could not be open and truthful about so critical a component of his identity, Baldwin reasoned, he could not be truthful about anything. "'Homosexual' is a hard word to accept," he told a Village friend one night, but in himself that acceptance was becoming easier to find.

Acceptance by others remained elusive, however, and for Baldwin, Greenwich Village—"where I quickly discovered that my existence was the punchline of a dirty joke"—had never been the bastion of tolerance it was reputed to be. Even in this neighborhood of artistic and social license, his sexual preference and especially his color—he was, he later recalled, one of only a handful of African Americans living in the Village at the time—made him a target, and he was regularly harassed: yelled at, chased by drunken men, thrown out of bars and restaurants, rousted by the police for no reason. At times, he said, when "walking past a group of whites, I sometimes felt so angry I wanted to go 'bam.'"

To his mind, the very fabric of American society worked to drag black people "under," and he worried that he might be swallowed up by the kind of hatred and despair that caused his "best friend," Eugene Worth, a young black man, to leap to his death from the George Washington Bridge in 1946. "I knew what was going to happen to me," Baldwin remembered in the interview he gave the *Paris Review* in 1984. "My luck was running out. I was going to jail, I was going to kill somebody or be killed." The same forces that had driven his friend to self-destruction were at work on himself: "Looking for a place to live. Looking for a job. You begin to doubt your judgment, you begin to doubt everything. You become imprecise. And that's when you're beginning to go under. You've been beaten, and it's been deliberate. The whole society has decided to make you *nothing*."

Worth's suicide illustrated to Baldwin more than just the perils of the country's noxious racial climate, for he suffered great personal guilt as well over his friend's death, wondering if his own insensitivity, insecurity, or confusion about his identity had led him to reject his friend's offer of love and contributed as much to his suicide as had societal pressures. The two had never been lovers, Baldwin would write two years before his own death, though he had come to wish that they had been, and he recalled an incident in which Worth, after humorously reviewing a list of girlfriends and describing the depth of his feelings for each, then said to Baldwin, "I wonder if I might be in love with you."

Though he did not respond to his friend's veiled declaration, the moment remained with Baldwin. "I wish I had heard him more clearly: an oblique confession is clearly a plea," he wrote in "Here Be Dragons." "But I was to hurt a great many people by being unable to imagine that anyone could possibly be in love with an ugly boy like me." In print, Baldwin would attribute his rejection of Worth to his own lack of self-esteem, but it is possible that it owed as much to his own confusion about his sexual identity. Their friendship was forged at a time when Baldwin, despite statements to the contrary, was still trying to resolve the question of his sexuality by engaging in relationships with women and even contemplating marriage as a final solution. Significantly, perhaps, Weatherby states that Baldwin threw the engagement ring he bought for Grace into the Hudson River "near where" Worth met his death.

The pain of Worth's death lingers in Baldwin's fiction as well. *Giovanni's Room* and *Another Country*, the two novels that follow *Go Tell It on the Mountain*, Baldwin's fictional exploration of his childhood and his family's history, both take as their themes the personal, emotional, and psychological consequences of failed, thwarted, or rejected love. In both novels, societal and personal pressure toward sexual conformity play an enormous role in the tragic events that unfold. In *Another Country*, a young black man named Rufus Scott kills himself by jumping from the George Washington Bridge; though the societal pressures that beat Rufus down are primarily connected with race, his best friend, Vivaldo Moore, who often professes his love for his lost friend, is left guilt ridden about his death, and there is clearly a measure of erotic attraction between the two, both of whom, in the course of the novel, are sexually involved with both women and men. At one point, before his death, Rufus even asks Vivaldo, "Have you ever wished you were queer?" Vivaldo concedes that he has in fact wished so, but that he is not, a response that Rufus concedes, but perhaps not entirely truthfully, is valid for himself as well.

Whether or not one reads Rufus's question as an "oblique confession" constituting a "plea"—it is made at a time of great emotional stress and is followed shortly by an even more anguished outburst ("I don't want to die") that is the only real clue Rufus gives as to the extremity of his emotional condition and the enormity of the act he is contemplating, and is, like his earlier declaration, not really heard for what it is by Vivaldo, who is "tired of Rufus's story" and "of friendship"—it is clear that both Rufus and Vivaldo are in varying degrees of confusion, if not denial, about their sexual natures and that component of their identity that is attracted to men. Though, earlier on, Rufus does return physically the love offered him by another male friend, Eric, he treats him "as nothing more than a hideous sexual deformity," a freak; later on, when it is all but too late, he concedes to himself that Eric had loved him. And despite his reply to Rufus, Vivaldo later (after Rufus's death) engages in an emotionally and physically satisfying (albeit brief) affair with Eric that is in some ways a surrogate for the missed opportunity with Rufus; he even confesses to Eric that on another night of tremendous emotional turmoil for Rufus, he had sensed that Rufus wanted him to approach him in bed, but that he had been unable to bring himself to.

Whether any of the love that eludes Rufus or is rejected by him might have proved sufficient to save him is impossible to say, for his despair arises as well from the way he, as a black man, is treated by society; but, Baldwin subtly points out, the fears and prejudices that act on and in individuals to prevent the fulfillment of love between members of the same sex are no less damning than those that separate the races, and are in some way connected. Both Vivaldo and Rufus engage in interracial love affairs with women; Vivaldo with Rufus's sister, Ida, after his death, and Rufus with Leona, a white woman from the South. Neither works out; guilt, fear, suspicion, mistrust, and anger, expressed individually as the result of seemingly inescapable personal, historical, and societal forces, act to drag the lovers apart; the gulf between black and white is still too wide. Although Leona's love for Rufus is genuine, he rejects and even brutalizes her, essentially because she is white; significantly, he uses "against her the very epithets he had used against Eric, and in the very same way, with the same roaring in his head and the same intolerable pressure in his chest."

In the earlier novel, *Giovanni's Room,* Baldwin makes the link between denial of one's sexual nature, the loss of love, and death even more explicit. Giovanni, an Italian bartender in Paris, comes to tragedy because of the failure of a love affair with David, a white American expatriate. David has spent his young lifetime trying to repress and deny his attraction to men, most recently by proposing marriage to a young woman, but while his girlfriend is away contemplating his proposal, he falls headlong in love upon meeting Giovanni. While unable to deny the depth and authenticity of his physical and emotional attachment to Giovanni (and Giovanni's for him), David is terrified, not so much by his feelings as by what other people would think, for he had decided long ago, after an adolescent sexual encounter with his best friend, "to allow no room in the universe for something which frightened and shamed me." David even concedes to himself at one point "that it was not really so strange, though voices deep within me boomed, For shame! For shame! that I should be so abruptly, so hideously entangled with a boy; what was strange was that this was but one tiny aspect of the dreadful human tangle occurring everywhere, without end, forever." Love is love, in other words, rare, precious, and frightening, and the consequences of rejecting it prove terrible: David cruelly abandons Giovanni, as he had cruelly rejected his childhood friend. Giovanni dies tragically, David is unable to endure a closeted life with his fiancée, and their relationship disintegrates when she discovers his secret. At the end of the novel, David, because of his lack of courage in acknowledging his identity, can anticipate only further misery and an even more profound loneliness. Try what he will, the physical desire within him will never abate, but because he is unable to accept the truth about himself, he will never be able to give or accept true love and so will know none, only a succession of affectionless physical encounters.

Judging by the fiction that it clearly inspired, it is evident that Worth's suicide had a profound effect on Baldwin. It is in their fiction that novelists express those concerns that are most central to their existence; the first two novels that Baldwin finished after Worth's suicide and the completion of his already-begun work-in-progress are both concerned with a death that results, at least in part, from a failure or inability to acknowledge the possibility of sexual love between men—a failure or inability that Baldwin was to acknowledge, though for reasons much different than those motivating his fictional characters, was a part of his relationship with Worth.

Whether Baldwin's inability or unwillingness to respond to Worth's "plea" had anything to do with his own attempt to resolve his anguish about his sexuality through marriage remains unknown (though art is also a kind of oblique confession, he wrote in his essay "The Northern Protestant," which was first published in 1960), but it is clear that questions about his identity—as a writer, as a black American, and as a man—continued to trouble him and inspired a difficult decision: to leave the United States. "I no longer felt I knew who I really was," he would tell Weatherby years later, "whether I was really black or white, really male or female, really talented or a fraud, really strong or merely stubborn. . . . I had to get my head together to survive and my only hope of doing that was to leave America." When asked years later in the *Paris Review* interview what had led him to leave the United States, Baldwin cited the general social conditions that then prevailed for blacks and Worth's suicide.

With the money that remained from his Rosenwald Foundation grant, most of which had gone to his mother, Baldwin bought a one-way airplane ticket for Paris. The city was a traditional haven of expatriate American artists, black and white, but in Baldwin's mind his destination was less important than the fact of his leaving. "It wasn't so much a matter of choosing France," he would tell Jordan Elgrably, the *Paris Review* interviewer, as "it was a matter of getting out of America."

He left New York on November 11, 1948, with just $40 in his pocket and no real prospect of earning any more. His last hours before leaving were spent in his family's Harlem apartment; he had, until the very last minute, been unable to bring himself to inform his family of his decision. When he broke the news, his youngest sister, five-year-old Paula Maria, began to cry uncontrollably. Seeing that he had made up his mind, his mother resigned herself to the idea and said little.

When it was time for him to go, she walked him downstairs in silence. She was stoic and reserved, and Baldwin searched his heart for the words to explain this drastic decision. He wanted to help her understand his burning desire to become a successful writer; to understand his confusion and his guilt and his fear and his sense of doom. "Once I had left the pulpit," he wrote years later in his introduction to *The Price of the Ticket,* "I had abandoned or betrayed my role in the community. . . . Once it became clear that I was not going to go to college, I became a kind of two-headed monstrosity of a problem. . . . There are few things more dreadful than dealing with a man who knows that he is going under, in his own eyes, and in the eyes of others. . . . I didn't want my Mama, or the kids, to see me like that." But he could not say a thing; in his own words, he fled. Without looking back, he dashed into a cab, to his plane, and off toward what he hoped to be a new beginning.

CHAPTER FOUR

A HARD WAY
TO GO

Richard Wright stands in front of a poster for an Argentine film version of his seminal novel, *Native Son,* in which he starred. "I don't think that Richard ever thought of me as one of his responsibilities," Baldwin wrote in "Alas, Poor Richard," "but he certainly seemed, often enough, to wonder just what he had done to deserve me."

Paris had long had a reputation as a place where black artists could flourish. In the 1920s the great African American actress, dancer, singer, and comedian Josephine Baker had made her mark as a performer on Paris stages, and France embraced her as its own. Many jazz musicians, among them the influential saxophonists Sidney Bechet and Coleman Hawkins, had found more appreciative audiences overseas and relocated, some temporarily, some permanently, to Paris. Black writers such as Frank Yerby, author of such best-selling novels as *The Foxes of Harrow,* and Chester Himes, who would become well known for his detective novels, including *Cotton Comes to Harlem,* made their homes in Paris, and, of course, Richard Wright had moved there in 1946.

But in 1948, the world capital of high culture was still suffering from the effects of its occupation by Nazi Germany in World War II. Many roads and bridges were still out; certain important buildings had been seriously damaged; food supplies and gasoline were still being rationed; and most of the city's residents got around on bicycles. Jobs were essentially unavailable for Americans, though in one sense the city's economic problems made it more attractive to expatriates: rent and food were both remarkably cheap.

Initially, Paris seemed to be the answer to Baldwin's prayers. Friends helped him find a cheap hotel, and though his $40 lasted just three days and his inability to speak French made finding employment unlikely, Baldwin found that his enormous reading, particularly of the 19th-century French novelist Honoré de Balzac, provided him with a certain understanding of "the way that country and its society works," to the extent that in some ways Paris seemed almost familiar to him. And in France, for the first time, the race consciousness developed in him in the United States seemed to disappear; it came as a pleasant surprise to him when someone asked whether a newly made acquaintance was black or white and Baldwin found that he either had not noticed or could not remember. (In an interview given to Kenneth Clark in 1963, Baldwin remembered a time in his homeland before such distinctions were made so important to him: When he returned from one of his first days of school, his mother asked him if the teacher had been colored or white, and Baldwin replied innocently, "A little bit colored and a little bit white, but she was about your color.") "It was a great revelation to me," Baldwin told Margaret Mead in 1971, "when I found myself finally in France among all kinds of very different people . . . different from anybody I had met in America. . . . I had come through *something,* shed a dying skin and was naked again."

Baldwin's friends took him to make the rounds of the cafés, restaurants, and bars where congregated the American colony of would-be writers, journalists, artists, and assorted bohemians, as well as the largest contingent, "students," most of them World War II veterans enjoying a continental experience on the small but secure income provided by the GI Bill. On his first day he was reacquainted at the Deux Magots café with Richard Wright, who hailed him with his customary greeting of "Hey boy." Though glad to see Wright, Baldwin would later profess to be disgusted by the company he kept in Paris—French intellectuals, including the philosophers Jean-Paul Sartre and Simone de Beauvoir, whom he believed treated Wright with unwarranted condescension.

Baldwin's disdain for the company Wright kept was only a portent of even greater disillusionment to come. Most members of the American colony had some regular source of income, however small, but Baldwin had none at all, and his relentless scrounging and borrowing—drinks, cigarettes, meals, rent money, places to sleep—alienated the goodwill of some of his acquaintances and wounded his pride. He worked briefly, as a messenger for an American patent attorney, but still money seemed to dislike him, and when he did have some he tended to be overly generous to friends and hangers-on. He had to sell his clothes, and even his typewriter, for food, and he soon felt the effects of missing so many meals and sleeping in poorly heated rooms: During the exceptionally cold first winter he spent in Paris he contracted pneumonia, surviving only through the generosity of a Corsican woman who owned the hotel where he was staying and who fed him, nursed him, and forgave his bills. Once he was back on his feet, the endless scuffling resumed; at times he was so desperate he sold himself for a night or two to the wealthy older patrons of gay bars.

Baldwin also came to recognize that the relative absence of racial prejudice that he experienced in Paris did not mean that French society was devoid of distinctions based on race or class. Paris had always had *les miserables*—the miserable, or wretched ones, as the novelist Victor Hugo had called them—and in Baldwin's time there the most wretched and outcast were the Arab immigrants from France's colony of Algeria in northern Africa. Baldwin befriended many Arabs and sometimes stayed in the Arab Quarter of the city, thereby coming to see how they were treated by other Parisians—"like dirt," he said. "In France," he said in an interview he gave to the *Black Scholar* in 1973, "the Algerian is the nigger."

Further understanding that poverty and powerlessness exist regardless of color came around Christmas of 1949, when Baldwin landed in a French prison for several days. In his essay "Equal in Paris," he attributes his jailing to a rather farcical misunderstanding about a stolen hotel bed sheet, although a fellow American expatriate writer, Herbert

The immortal "empress of the blues," Bessie Smith, exerted a greater influence on Baldwin's work than any other black musician. Baldwin wrote that in Europe, Smith's music helped "reconcile" him to his identity as a black American.

Gold, suggested to Weatherby that Baldwin had been picked up by the French police in the course of one of their periodic roustings of gay bars.

The reason for the arrest is ultimately less important than the lesson Baldwin draws from it in "Equal in Paris." According to that account, after about a week of imprisonment, Baldwin was brought to trial, where his account of the stolen hotel sheet aroused great mirth in the courtroom and the charges were dropped. But Baldwin was not amused; the laughter of the officials and onlookers in the courtroom reminded him of the laughter and scorn he was trying to escape by coming to Paris, and although he knew he was not being laughed at for quite the same reasons that he had been at home, it galled him nonetheless. "This laughter," he wrote, "is the laughter of those who consider themselves to be at a safe remove from all the wretched, for whom the pain of the living is not real. I had heard it so often in my native land that I had resolved to find a place where I would never hear it any more. In some deep, black, stony, and liberating way, my life, in my own eyes, began during that first year in Paris, when it was borne in on me that this laughter is universal and can never be stilled."

In such unsettled circumstances, it proved difficult for Baldwin to write as much as he needed or wanted to. To his dismay, he discovered upon his arrival in Paris that he had accidentally left his manuscript of *Crying Holy* behind, forcing him to begin the novel again. His progress on the work still dissatisfied him, as did his efforts on another project he had begun in New York, a novel about gay life in Greenwich Village called alternately *Ignorant Armies* or *So Long at the Fair*.

Baldwin was able to complete one project, an essay he had promised the *Partisan Review* that ran first in a French-run English magazine called *Zero*. The article, entitled "Everybody's Protest Novel," won him no small amount of notice, but it cost him the friendship and support of his patron, Richard Wright.

The essay was essentially Baldwin's critical reconsideration of the favorite novel of his childhood, *Uncle Tom's Cabin*. His opinion of the novel had changed a great deal since the days when he had read and reread it so feverishly that his mother was moved to take it from him. Then, it had held a strange fascination for him, but now it seemed more like a model of the pitfalls that as an aspiring young writer (and most especially as a young *black* writer, which was, as he had already seen, to risk being automatically made a spokesman for the collective black point of view) he should struggle to avoid. "*Uncle Tom's Cabin* is a very bad novel," he bluntly states near the opening of his essay, for the reason that Stowe is less a writer than a propagandist, less an artist than an abolitionist, and her book is less a novel than a political tract, a catalog of the violence and horrors of slavery, and a badly written and sentimental one, devoid of fully developed characters, at that. The story and the characters and the horrific violence of Stowe's novel are used not to illuminate any truth about human character or American history but to serve a political end. Though that end might be honorable and just, according to Baldwin—"her book was not intended to do anything more than prove that slavery was wrong"—it did not make her book art, which in Baldwin's eyes serves an even more important purpose. While protest novels such as Stowe's, Baldwin argues, prove a point—in this case, that slavery is wrong—works of art pose and attempt to answer truthfully even more important questions, such as "what it was, after all, that moved [white] people to such deeds."

Stowe's characters, Baldwin finds, are less complex, fully rounded human beings than they are categorizations. A human being is not just, as Baldwin feels protest novelists such as Stowe would make him or her, a "member of a Society or a Group or a deplorable conundrum to be explained by Science. He is . . . something more than that, something resolutely indefinable, unpredictable. In overlooking, denying, evading his complexity—which is nothing more than the disquieting complexity of ourselves—we are diminished and we perish; only within the web of ambiguity, paradox, this hunger, danger, darkness, can we find at once ourselves and the power that will free us from ourselves." To create art, Baldwin says, is the true business of the novelist; to do otherwise is to reduce people to cardboard characters and to reduce the truth.

Baldwin's discussion of *Uncle Tom's Cabin* runs for more than nine of the less than ten-and-a-half pages that his essay occupies in *Notes of a Native Son*. In the last 41 lines of the work, he turns his attention to Bigger Thomas, the ill-fated protagonist of Wright's *Native Son,* whom he says is "Uncle Tom's descendant, flesh of his flesh, so exactly opposite a portrait that, when the books are placed together, it seems that the contemporary Negro novelist and the dead New England woman are locked together in a deadly timeless battle." Though, as was true of Stowe's novel, Baldwin had no real argument with the point Wright was trying to make with *Native Son,* he felt nonetheless that Bigger, like Uncle Tom, was less a character than a categorization, a product of the oppressive social conditions so pitilessly depicted by Wright who is never allowed by his creator the possibility of transcendence.

What made the brutal, murderous, raping Bigger so terrifying to the readers of *Native Son,* and so ominous in his implications for American society, was precisely what Baldwin objected to: the seeming impossibility, given the social and economic conditions in which he comes to maturity, of his turning out any other way. America did create Biggers, Baldwin well knew, and damaged others from similar backgrounds in a thousand different ways; he knew as well (from his own experience, for one, although he avoided saying so) that others, in similar conditions, found a way to forge a different sort of life for themselves, a possibility that Wright's fictional treatment, by implication, excluded. Elsewhere, Baldwin would liken Bigger to a kind of Frankenstein's monster created by America. America was to blame, Baldwin would agree, but Wright's protest-novelist's approach was too reductive; in excluding other possibilities for Bigger, *Native Son* served ultimately, despite the author's contrary intent, to reinforce white America's demonization of blacks. "The failure of the protest novel," Baldwin concludes, "lies in its rejection of life, the human being, the denial of his beauty, dread, power, in its insistence that is his categorization alone which is real and which cannot be transcended."

It was the the final 41 lines of "Everybody's Protest Novel" that caught the attention of most readers, including Wright, who interpreted it as an attack. On the very day that *Zero* was published, the established writer and his protégé met by chance in a café, and Wright lashed out at Baldwin, accusing him of betraying his trust, of trying to sabotage his reputation and the reputation of his novel. Over and over again Baldwin denied that his intention was to injure. "It never occurred to me," Baldwin said in an interview years later. "Maybe I was being very cunning to myself—but it never occurred to myself that it could be read as an attack on Richard. I thought I was being a bright honors student.

I thought we could have a discussion about that. His reaction made me reexamine everything."

That "reexamination" took the form of an even lengthier essay, "Many Thousands Gone," first published in 1951, in which Baldwin expanded on the brief criticisms he had offered in "Everybody's Protest Novel." Though Baldwin and Wright met again on numerous occasions, their relationship was never truly healed. In his final essay on Wright, "Alas, Poor Richard," published in 1961 not long after Wright's death, Baldwin, in attempting a kind of posthumous reconciliation and repentance, nonetheless manages to extend his criticism of Wright from the literary to the personal.

Numerous biographers and critics have speculated on the reasons why Baldwin behaved so cruelly toward a man who had been so genuinely kind toward him. Although, according to friends, Baldwin's wit and intelligence could often be scathing, he was rarely cruel and more often generous. Baldwin himself provides the clearest explanation in "Alas, Poor Richard," where, while somewhat disingenuously proclaiming his surprise that Wright interpreted the first essay as an attack (and conspicuously avoiding mention of the second), he almost simultaneously admits that Wright was justified in feeling hurt, and that he, Baldwin, had been wrong in hurting him (though not in the truth of what he had written). While Wright had treated him like a friend, Baldwin had found true friendship between them impossible, but not because, as Wright believed, he did not like the older man. Instead, it was Wright's unprecedented stature as a black writer, his artistic success, his importance to Baldwin as a literary figure and model, that prevented a true friendship from developing. "We had not become friends," Baldwin wrote in "Alas, Poor Richard," "because I was really too young to be his friend and adored him too much and was too afraid of him." To Baldwin, Wright's artistic achievement and importance were so great that "he became . . . alas! my father."

From Baldwin, such a statement is immensely revealing. Just as it had been necessary for him to reach an understanding of his father's bitterness and hatred and anger and religion, and then reject it, in order for him to discover his own identity as a human being, so was it necessary for him, as a young, intelligent, questioning, ever-so-ambitious young writer, to come to a critical understanding of Wright's literary work—to reject it, in short—in order to find his own literary way. To a certain extent, Bigger Thomas is the literary embodiment of the bitterness that finally ate David Baldwin up, of the "fever," the "rage in the blood," that Baldwin himself had first contracted in New Jersey, and Baldwin's treatment of Wright is therefore part of the same process of understanding and rejection—an attempt, in his life and in his art, to

Marlon Brando, seen here in a publicity still for the 1951 film *A Streetcar Named Desire,* became a good friend of Baldwin's during their bohemian days in Greenwich Village in the 1940s. The two were often reunited in the 1960s at civil rights rallies and remained lifelong friends.

transcend bitterness and hatred and reach a deeper truth—that he would chart in "Notes of a Native Son."

"No American Negro exists who does not have his private Bigger Thomas living in the skull," Baldwin wrote in "Many Thousands Gone," and, elsewhere in the same essay, "There is, I should think, no Negro living in America who has not felt, briefly or for long periods . . . simple, naked, and unanswerable hatred; who has not wanted to smash any white face he may encounter in a day." Certainly, Baldwin had; such feelings had nearly overwhelmed him in both New Jersey and New York and helped drive him to France to discover who he was, as a person and as a writer. But what Wright had failed to illuminate, Baldwin felt, was what he termed alternately the "precarious" and "paradoxical adjustment" that blacks were forced to make to that justified inner rage in order to live. His father's failure to do so had destroyed him, and Baldwin had rejected that failing, had made an adjustment that would allow him to find his own way as a person, as he would explain in "Notes of a Native Son." Bigger failed also to do so, denied an opportunity, Baldwin believed, through the artistic failing of his creator, and so he rejected those failings as well, in order to find the way to his own artistic truth.

Both rejections were necessary to Baldwin's emerging understanding of himself as an individual and as an artist. But whereas, in "Notes of a Native Son" (which would not be written for several more years), Baldwin was able to beautifully articulate a process of understanding of his father's life that enabled him to reject those destructive elements that threatened to harm his own existence without finally, in fact, rejecting his father—the essay is ultimately as much reconciliation as rejection, a recognition of how much its writer shared with his father—his rejection of *Native Son* as a literary model was less graceful. Wright, for one thing, was still alive, and Baldwin conceded in "Alas, Poor Richard" that his treatment of his onetime patron was "monstrously egotistical." What had been necessary for Baldwin on an artistic level, in his commitment to his emerging vision of artistic truth, was on a personal level, savage, failing to take into consideration the very real feelings Wright had shown for him. To Baldwin, Wright's fictional achievement was so monumental, and so critical to his own understanding of himself as a person and as a writer, that he could not expect to advance with his own novels until he had come to grips with *Native Son*; any understanding that he reached about that novel he was then obligated to express truthfully, in adherence to his credo of artistic responsibility. All this he expected Wright, as a fellow artist, to understand; to see that this very act of criticism was in one way a tribute to the greatness of *Native Son*—"the most powerful and celebrated statement we have yet had of what it means to be a Negro in America"—and to the achievement of its creator.

But Wright, Baldwin wrote in "Alas, Poor Richard," "saw clearly enough, far more clearly than I had dared to allow myself to see, what I had done: I had used his work as a kind of springboard into my own. His work was a roadblock in my road, the sphinx, really, whose riddles I had to answer before I could become myself. I thought confusedly then, and feel very definitely now, that this was the greatest tribute I could have paid him. But it is not an easy tribute to bear and I do not know how I will take it when my time comes. For, finally, Richard was hurt because I had not given him any credit for any human feelings or failings."

As if to further emphasize his artistic independence, in Paris, Baldwin first declared his enduring artistic passion for the work of Henry James, the American expatriate writer of the late 19th and early 20th century, whose artistic method and concerns could not have been further removed from Wright's. As a protest novelist, Baldwin felt, Wright was primarily interested in political and social ends, whereas in James's greatest novels—*The Portrait of a Lady, The Wings of the Dove, The Golden Bowl,* and *The Ambassadors*—political and social issues play no role whatsoever. The scion of an extremely wealthy New York family, James left the United States for England in 1876 and eventually became a British subject. Most of his characters are from the uppermost echelons of American and European society, and his most important novels take place in the mansions, country homes, drawing rooms, and villas of the very rich; there is not a black character in all of his fiction. The dominant themes in the four novels are the contrast between American innocence, youth, energy, and wealth and European sophistication, age, culture, and greed, as played out in the betrayal of love for money. Although, in the bare bones of their outlines, the plots of James's novels are exceedingly simple—frameworks, really, for James to explore the consciousness of his characters—the books themselves are not. James is less concerned with events than with their perception; his famous prose style, elaborate yet precise, with its elegant yet labyrinthine sentences and extremely long paragraphs, in which every thought and idea seems to be subjected to endless refinements, subtleties, and qualifications, serves to delineate the process by which the central character in each of the novels comes to understanding and makes his or her moral choices.

James's influence on Baldwin is evident in several ways. Away from the land of his birth, James was able to reach a clearer understanding of the United States, and he discovered the great theme of his fiction; Baldwin had come to Paris to finish the process of determining who he was, and as the essays he would write from the Paris years (those collected in *Notes of a Native Son*) illustrate, he was concerned in his own thinking with the role his homeland had played in shaping that identity. James was more interested in consciousness and perception than in events or action and found a style that embodied his concerns; in *Crying Holy* (and the novels that follow), Baldwin, too, was less concerned with plot than with trying to discover a language to portray singular and extremely complex states of mind in his characters, especially his protagonist, John Grimes. In that effort, Baldwin would say, "James was my key." Wright's style in *Native Son,* for example, is terse and spare and would have been spectacularly unsuited to describe the flood of thoughts and emotions that John experiences during his night on the threshing floor. Though Baldwin's fictional style, as it was soon to be exhibited, is uniquely his own, James certainly helped demonstrate to him the ways in which language could be used not just to convey a character's thoughts and emotions but to portray the process by which those thoughts and emotions are formed.

If James was to provide the "key" that would allow Baldwin to understand how to write his novel, another new passion would provide the emotional security and material circumstances that would allow him to finish it. Baldwin met Lucien Happersberger, a tall, slim, attractive, 17-year-old Swiss runaway who aspired to be an artist, near the end of 1949, in a seedy bar, called La Reine Blanche, frequented by what Baldwin termed "ambivalent men." Baldwin had continued to engage in relationships with both women and men, but the effect of his meeting Happersberger was dramatic. "I starved in Paris for a while, but I learned something," Baldwin later wrote. "For one thing I fell in love. Or, more accurately, I realized, and accepted for the first time that love was not merely a general human possibility, nor merely the disaster it had

Baldwin's lifelong friend Lucien Happersberger, whom he first met in Paris in 1949. Happersberger disappointed Baldwin by marrying; Baldwin was "tortured by the fact that Lucien had a son and that kind of relationship," said a mutual friend. Even so, he agreed to be godfather to the boy, who was named after him.

71

so often, by then, been for me—according to me—nor was it something that happened to other people, like death, nor was it merely a mortal danger: it was among *my* possibilities, for here it was, breathing and belching beside me, and it was the key to life."

Happersberger, who had no source of income and was living on his good looks and charm, also engaged in relationships with individuals of both sexes, many of them as a means of financial support. Although he and Baldwin became lovers for a time, according to Happersberger it was their friendship, which would endure to the end of Baldwin's life, that was the true basis of their relationship. For Baldwin, Lucien seems to have been the great love of his life, but his young friend did not share his dream of sharing a life together. "Jimmy was very romantic," Happersberger later told Campbell. "He had a dream of settling down." Baldwin would later tell people that he and Lucien had lived together as lovers in Paris, but according to Happersberger that was never the case. The two did usually meet every day, to pool their money and figure out a way to get something to eat, but both continued to be involved with other people as well, and in 1952 Happersberger got married for the first of several times. Still, their friendship endured. "We were buddies," Happersberger told Campbell. "We accepted each other exactly as we were. That's rare."

By the end of 1951, the pressure of scrambling for work and trying to finish his novel had brought Baldwin to the brink of emotional collapse, too few meals, too many cigarettes, and too much drinking imperiled his physical health, and the endless socializing that characterized expatriate life in Paris had become counterproductive. Sensing that his friend needed to get out of Paris for a time, Happersberger arranged for them to use his family's chalet in the tiny Swiss village of Loeche-les-Bains, 5,000 feet up in the Alps.

For Baldwin, Loeche-les-Bains could not have been more exotic or remote, both culturally and geographically. None of the 600 villagers had ever before seen a black man, and they would approach him on the street to rub his hair or touch his skin, arousing in Baldwin a series of conflicting emotions, as he explained in his essay "Stranger in the Village." The landscape of the region, Baldwin wrote in that same essay, was "absolutely forbidding, mountains towering on all four sides, ice and snow as far as the eye can reach."

Living on the 50 francs Lucien's father sent every week, Baldwin soon recouped his good health, and in three months, to the music of two Bessie Smith records played again and again, he was able to complete the novel that he had been trying to write for eight long years. The autobiographical story of John Grimes and his family now had a new title: *Go Tell It on the Mountain,* an allusion both to the black spiritual of the same name and the surroundings to which Baldwin had come in order to tell his story. On February 2, 1952, Baldwin mailed his novel to an agent in New York, Helen Strauss. Several weeks later she sent word: the esteemed publisher Alfred A. Knopf was very interested in the book and had made an offer. Could Baldwin come to New York?

Of course he could, but for one minor problem: the overjoyed first novelist was, as usual, flat broke, with no money for passage across the Atlantic. Fortunately, an old friend from Baldwin's bohemian days in Greenwich Village was in Paris, and Baldwin went to see him. Since the days when the two of them were struggling young artists together in New York City, Marlon Brando had enjoyed a somewhat greater degree of success as an actor than Baldwin had as a writer. Brando's turn as the brutish Stanley Kowalski in Tennessee Williams's play *A Streetcar Named Desire* had been the sensation of the 1947 Broadway season and had made him the hottest, hippest actor in America. Baldwin's admiration for the actor, as an artist and as a person, was immense, as he later told Weatherby: "I had never met any white man like Marlon. He was obviously immensely talented—a real creative force—and totally unconventional and independent, a beautiful cat. Race truly meant nothing to him. . . . He was contemptuous of anyone who discriminated in any way. Very attractive to both women and men, he gave me the feeling that reports I was ugly had been much exaggerated." In Paris, Brando lent Baldwin $500, which the writer used to book passage on a ship bound for New York, the *Ile de France,* in April 1952. After four years of struggle, of seeking himself in a foreign land, he was heading home in triumph.

CHAPTER FIVE

MY SOUL
LOOKS BACK AND
WONDERS

Though Knopf enjoyed a lofty reputation as a publisher of books of great importance and high quality, and its interest in Baldwin's novel could thereby be interpreted by the writer as a very real indication of the quality of his manuscript, Baldwin found his experience with the company disillusioning. The amount of money he was offered for the book—$1,000—was not tremendous, and the nature of the changes his editor suggested that he make to the manuscript made it clear to him that the man had not understood the novel very well. Back in Paris, Baldwin complied with the editorial suggestions and completed a revision, which was in his publisher's hands by July, but he later felt he should have been forceful and resisted. He likened dealing with editors to "being in a lion's den." Most of the suggested changes had to do with reducing the

Baldwin at work. Like most young writers, he was hungry for success, but he would find fame to be a mixed blessing.

amount of religious language in the work; although Capouya recalled reading an early version of the work in which John Grimes declared his homosexuality at the end, it is less than certain that this was the version Baldwin presented to Knopf, and there is no evidence that the publisher objected to the homoerotic content of the book. Certainly, the implied homoerotic overtones of John's relationship with Elisha, a slightly older young minister, remain in the published version of *Go Tell It on the Mountain*.

The final version of *Go Tell It on the Mountain* may not have conformed to Baldwin's ideal, but when the novel was published in May 1953 critics found it admirable nonetheless. The *Saturday Review* called it "masterful." A reviewer in *Commonweal* wrote: "His work has a majestic sense of the failings of men and their ability to work through the misery to salvation." The *New York Times* review noted that it was "written with great intensity of feeling." Others called it "poetic and true." So positive was the attention accorded his first novel that Baldwin received a fellowship from the Guggenheim Memorial Foundation—a substantial, no-strings-attached cash grant.

Following the publication of *Go Tell It on the Mountain,* Baldwin decided to further explore, in the form of a play, the sanctified world of the storefront churches he had known as a boy. He had long been interested in drama as an artistic form and had even taken some acting classes during his days in the Village. In several months, he produced a play, *The Amen Corner,* which concerned the relationship between a powerful spiritual leader—very much like Mother Horn of the Pentecostal Assembly—and her rebellious son, but when he sent it to his agent, Helen Strauss, she was somewhat less than encouraging about its commercial potential. A first novel was one thing, Baldwin recalled Strauss telling him, but "the American theater was not exactly clamoring for plays on obscure aspects of Negro life," a conclusion with which Baldwin agreed practically—writing the play seemed a "desperate and even rather irresponsible act," he later conceded—but, with customary singlemindedness, rejected artistically. She advised him to concentrate on magazine writing instead; meanwhile his publishers pressed for a new novel.

Baldwin was working on a new novel—an as yet imperfectly conceived piece that would eventually evolve into both *Giovanni's Room* and *Another Country*—but his next published work would be a collection of essays. *Notes of a Native Son* consisted of five old essays—the most important being the two dealing with Richard Wright and *Native Son*—and five new ones that Baldwin would write before its publication in 1955. Of this new material, the most important was the essay that gave the collection its title, one of the most moving, eloquent, and intelligent pieces of writing he would ever produce. The title of the collection and of the essay is both a tribute to Wright's seminal novel and a subtle challenge. I, too, am a native son, Baldwin is saying, one with an identity quite different from Bigger Thomas's. The title reflects as well Baldwin's growing awareness that, despite his expatriate status, he was still very much an American. With his increasing income affording him greater freedom to travel, Baldwin was spending more and more time in the United States; much to his surprise, he would write in "A Question of Identity," a later essay, in Paris he had "proved . . . to be as American as any Texas G.I." Overall, despite the wide range of subject matter covered in *Notes of a Native Son,* from movie reviews, Wright's novel, and anti-Semitism in Harlem to his father's death and his own life as an expatriate in Paris, the primary recurring theme is one that would preoccupy Baldwin throughout much of the rest of his written work, particularly his essays: his struggle to form and maintain an individual and artistic identity in a society that puts very little value on the life and contributions of its black citizens. As would be true of virtually all of his essays, Baldwin invariably uses the ostensible subject matter of the piece—his prison stay in Paris, a review of a movie opera—as a springboard to an examination of the subject that really interests him: the effects of the poisonous racial climate of the United States on the black American individual.

Interestingly, one of the few of Baldwin's early essays that he did not include in *Notes of a Native Son* was an article called "Preservation of Innocence," which first appeared in the Summer 1949 issue of *Zero.* The piece is one of the very few essays in which Baldwin explicitly addresses the topic of homosexuality; though his reasons for not including it can only be speculated upon, it must be presumed that he felt the work to be not entirely successful—it was originally intended to be the first of a series of such pieces—and was not made wary by the controversial nature of the subject matter, as he would soon prove himself fearless in that regard. Though "Preservation of Innocence" does lack the clarity of thought, elegance of language, and beauty of design of his best pieces, such as "Notes of a Native Son," it is interesting nonetheless; in it, Baldwin disparages the commonly held American notion that homosexuality is impermissible because it is somehow "unnatural."

"A phenomenon as old as mankind," Baldwin writes, can hardly be considered unnatural. He suggests instead that America's fear of homosexuality is related to a greater overall fear of sex in general, as revealed in a debased notion of the relationship between the sexes and a corresponding unwillingness to accept the complexity of human behavior and possibilities. Any true understanding of human sexual behavior, Baldwin argues, must acknowledge what he calls the "merciless paradox" to which "an immense proportion of the myth, legend, and literature of the world is devoted": that it is impossible to "decide, of our multiple human attributes, which are masculine and which are feminine." Once again, Baldwin argues that any human being is much more complex than whatever category he might be placed in—be that black, white, slave, free, male, female, gay, or straight. He then cites the prevalence of violent, tough-guy types in contemporary American fiction, particularly in the detective novels of Raymond Chandler and especially James M. Cain, as evidence of America's unrealistic ideals of masculinity; denigrates the few American novels that had attempted to treat the issue of male homosexuality, and concludes that no "worthwhile novel" will ever be written about male love so long as gay men are treated as a "type" and not as individuals enacting one of the infinite variations of the incalculably complex human drama.

When *Notes of a Native Son* was published by the Beacon Press in 1955, it was generally recognized as a small classic. The most important praise came from the undisputed dean of African American literature, Langston Hughes, the most accomplished of the poets of the Harlem

A playbill for the May 1955 Howard University
production of Baldwin's drama *The Amen Corner*.
Like his great literary inspiration Henry James,
Baldwin was to find all his experiences in the
theater quite disappointing.

Renaissance. Though Hughes had written rather negatively about *Go Tell It on the Mountain,* calling it "a low-down story in a velvet bag," he was full of praise for the new collection, characterizing its author as a "straight-from-the-shoulder writer" and the essays themselves as "superb . . . thought-provoking, tantalizing, irritating, abusing, and amusing." Hughes's praise was qualified, however, and Baldwin was annoyed that the celebrated writer felt compelled to voice his opinion that the newcomer was not yet a "great artist in writing." In Hughes's mind, Baldwin was too obsessed with racial issues; he urged him to "look at life purely as himself and for himself."

Baldwin enjoyed a smaller sort of triumph that same year, when *The Amen Corner* was performed at Howard University in Washington, D.C., under the direction of Owen Dodson, an African American poet, playwright, and professor. At Dodson's request, Baldwin traveled to Washington to help the Howard University Players rehearse the play. Though Baldwin, sensitive about his own lack of university training, was a bit intimidated at the prospect of working with college students, he was put at ease by the respectful treatment of the students, and he found he liked the university setting. In late-night sessions, the students even educated him a little bit about the nascent civil rights movement in the South. The play ran for 10 nights in mid-May 1955 and was extremely well received by the college community; Lucien and some of Baldwin's brothers and sisters were in attendance on opening night, and Baldwin pronounced the entire experience "fantastic and wonderful." Still, he was disappointed that the production did not arouse greater interest, particularly from Broadway producers.

Even greater disappointment would come with the completion of his second novel, *Giovanni's Room.* Though perhaps not Baldwin's best novel, this somewhat melodramatic story of male sexual love and betrayal required considerable artistic and personal courage on his part. Daring to write from the perspective of a white American and to portray gay love in exactly the same way that straight love was dealt with in the novels of the day, Baldwin found himself rejected by both his agent and his publisher. Helen Strauss advised him to "burn" the manuscript—the two never worked together again—and Knopf rejected the novel as "repugnant." Even by the considerably more restrained standards of the 1950s, the book is discreet; it contains no explicit sex scenes, but apparently just the concept of a love story between males was too much for the Knopf editors to bear. To Baldwin, the contretemps was proof that the United States was, as he would put it in "Down at the Cross," an "antisexual" nation and confirmation of the accuracy of his portrayal of David, the blond, all-American narrator of the story, who rejects any hope for his own future happiness and (indirectly, and albeit unintentionally) helps sentence Giovanni to death because of his inability to admit to himself that he is attracted to men.

To Baldwin, it was the possibility of genuine love between two people, not the gender of the lovers, that was important. "Homosexual, bisexual, heterosexual are 20th-century terms which, for me, really have very little meaning," he would tell an interviewer in 1965. "I've never myself, in watching myself and watching other people, watching life, been able to discern exactly where the barriers were. Life being what life is, passion being what passion is. And learning being what that is. . . . It seems to me, in the first place, that if one's to live at all, one's certainly got to get rid of the labels." In a later interview, in 1969, he expressed the opinion that "American males are the only people in the world who are willing to go on the needle before they go to bed with one another." Such fears, he would indicate elsewhere, indicated less homophobia than a fear of life: "Everybody's journey is individual. You don't know with whom you're going to fall in love. . . . If you fall in love with a boy, you fall in love with a boy." At a time when many Americans, including those in the scientific and medical establishment, regarded homosexuality as something to be cured through therapy and various different kinds of treatment, Baldwin believed that "the fact that many Americans consider it a disease says more about them than it says about homosexuality."

As if to confirm Baldwin's beliefs about the peculiarly American fears of the subject matter, an English publisher, Michael Joseph, agreed to take *Giovanni's Room* without reservation. An American publisher, Dial Press, then agreed to take the book as well, and it appeared in both countries to great acclaim, with some of the foremost literary critics in the United States singing Baldwin's praises. Edmund Wilson, without a doubt the country's preeminent man of letters, told Alfred Kazin, himself a prominent critic, that Baldwin was one of the best young writers to come on the scene in a long time. His old editor and patron

Philip Rahv remarked in print that "it has been a long time since I have read anything as good by a younger American writer." The reviewer for the *New York Times,* the esteemed literary scholar Granville Hicks, wrote that "Mr. Baldwin writes of these matters [the love affair between

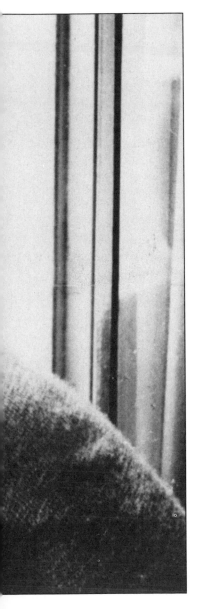

A publicity photo of Baldwin that was used in the promotion of *Giovanni's Room.* The book was dedicated to Lucien Happersberger and included as its epigraph a quotation from a Walt Whitman poem, "I am the man, I suffered, I was there"—an indication, perhaps, that the author's relationship with Lucien provided him with some insight into the pain suffered by Giovanni when his love is rejected.

Giovanni and David] with an unusual degree of candor and yet with such dignity and intensity that he is saved from sensationalism." The critic Mark Schorer described the novel as "beautifully written" and "nearly heroic." For Baldwin, the reviews confirmed the wisdom of following his own artistic judgment. "Always make up your own mind," he told Weatherby. "You just can't afford to let other people give you their evaluation of your own book."

The artistic and critical success of *Giovanni's Room* did not translate to true personal happiness for Baldwin. He was often seriously depressed that Lucien had not wanted the same things from their relationship that he had, and he tried to relieve his sadness with a series of desultory affairs, which served only to aggravate his loneliness. Although he was by no means wealthy, his income level had risen considerably since his days of being down and out in Paris, enough to allow him to travel at will back and forth between Paris and the United States and even to enjoy European retreats on the islands of Majorca and Corsica, and with an assured market for his essays, magazine articles, and novels, he could be reasonably certain of earning an adequate living in the near future. A certain amount of money and fame made companionship easy to come by, and certainly beat being "poor and ugly and obscure," but Baldwin, for all the gregariousness, camaraderie, and generosity he displayed in the Paris cafés, where he had become a most popular figure, wished for something deeper. "It does not take long, after all," he wrote in the essay "The Male Prison," which appears in his collection *Nobody Knows My Name,* "to discover that sex is only sex, that there are few things on earth more futile or more deadening than a meaningless round of conquests." For a time, he thought he found what he was looking for in an affair with a young black jazz musician from Harlem, a vibraphonist named Arnold to whom he was introduced in Greenwich Village by Lucien and with whom he lived for a time in Paris, but after several months Baldwin broke off the relationship. Friends believed that he continued to long for Lucien; others observed that although he spoke often of his desire for lasting love, his intellectual and temperamental restlessness made it difficult for him to remain satisfied with any situation for long.

A greater dissatisfaction was at work in him as well. After nearly nine years abroad, Baldwin had come to realize, as he would put it in the introduction to *Nobody Knows My Name,* that his "life in Europe was ending." He had come to Paris, he would say many times, because he did not know who he was, only to discover one certain thing about his identity: be he a black man or a gay man—and he insisted, in his opposition to such reductive labels, that he was "merely" neither—he was also an American. "I found myself, willy-nilly, alchemized into an American the moment I touched French soil," he would write in "A Fly in Buttermilk." Although in France he had to a great extent been able to shed the barrier of skin color, which in America had helped prevent him from resolving the question of his identity, "it turned out," he wrote in the introduction to *Nobody Knows My Name,* "that the question of who I was was not solved because I had removed myself from the social forces which menaced me . . . these forces had become interior, and I had dragged them across the ocean with me. The question of who I was had at last become a personal question, and the answer was to be found in me." He had gone to Europe to obtain a clearer vision of himself—a writer's subject "is himself," he wrote—and to become a writer. Having succeeded in both, it was now time to return home. The process of understanding himself, he had come to see, was a lifelong one, but his identity as an American was immutable, and he could no longer explore that subject from abroad.

CHAPTER SIX

DOWN AT
THE CROSS

Baldwin and civil rights
leader Bayard Rustin (left) at
a press conference in New
York City in the early 1960s.
A longtime activist who had
been involved in civil rights
work since the early 1930s,
Rustin became a valued
lieutenant to Martin Luther
King, Jr., and organized the
March on Washington. Still,
he was sometimes regarded
by its leaders as a liability to
the movement because of his
homosexuality and an earlier
arrest on "morals" charges.

If, as Baldwin had determined, his primary subject as
a writer was to be himself and his identity as an
American, then the need for him to return to the
United States in 1957 was obvious, for at that time
black Americans were engaged in a revolutionary
movement that would profoundly alter the character
of American society. Goaded and then convinced by
decades of legal efforts on the part of the National
Association for the Advancement of Colored People
(NAACP), the federal courts had shown an increasing
willingness to consider the constitutionality of segregation, culminating in the Supreme Court's 1954
landmark ruling in *Brown* v. *Board of Education*. Made
newly hopeful by the ruling and inspired by the
solitary, spontaneous action of a woman named Rosa
Parks, who refused to give up her bus seat to a white
passenger, blacks in Montgomery, Alabama, organized
under the leadership of the city's black clergy, including a charismatic young preacher named Martin

Luther King, Jr., to protest segregation on the city's buses. Their 11-month boycott of the city bus lines ended in total victory in November 1956 and inspired numerous other nonviolent challenges to segregation throughout the South, which were met by whites with staunch opposition, including violence, lynchings, and increased activity on the part of such white supremacist organizations as the Ku Klux Klan and the newly formed White Citizens' Councils. The civil rights movement was not a subject that Baldwin could write about from Europe. In the years to come, Baldwin would define his artistic mission as "bearing witness," which he said, "doesn't mean I saw it. It means I was there." One could not bear witness to the events unfolding in the American South from abroad.

With a commission from *Harper's* magazine for an article, Baldwin arrived in September 1957 in Charlotte, North Carolina, where, to comply with federally mandated integration of schools, officials had come up with a plan whereby four black schoolchildren—one to a school—would attend classes at formerly all-white institutions. As Baldwin described in his article "A Hard Kind of Courage" (published in *Nobody Knows My Name* as "A Fly in Buttermilk"), the black students left for school in the morning with the threat of violence hanging over their heads and sometimes found their entrance to the school building blocked by a gauntlet of white students; a black schoolgirl, Dorothy Counts, the daughter of a Presbyterian minister, was stoned and spat upon and eventually abandoned her attempt at integration. Though the scene was less tense than a similar situation in Little Rock, Arkansas, which he visited a couple of weeks later and where for several days the National Guard blocked the entrance of nine black students to formerly all-white Central High School (the students were eventually escorted to class by U.S. Army paratroopers), Baldwin was enormously impressed by the lonely, silent strength and courage of the Charlotte students, especially a boy named Gus Roberts, on whom his piece focused.

From Charlotte, Baldwin went on to Atlanta, Georgia, where he met Martin Luther King for the first time. King's charisma, dignity, and intelligence greatly impressed him, as did his message of nonviolence and love. Blacks must not protest out of hatred, King preached; they must find a way to love even their oppressors, to redeem their oppressors with love. It was a message much in keeping with Baldwin's own determination to liberate himself from the bitterness in his own heart, and one that he would develop at great length in his own writing, particularly *The Fire Next Time*. The success of the movement so far and the spirit of determination and solidarity developed among the blacks in the South meant that "segregation is dead," King told the writer. Baldwin agreed but predicted that its demise would be protracted and costly. "The question is just how long, how violent and how expensive the funeral is going to be," he responded. In Montgomery, Alabama, the "Cradle of the Confederacy" and the birthplace of the civil rights movement, Baldwin heard King preach at the Dexter Avenue Baptist Church and witnessed firsthand the damage to King's home done by bombs hurled by white racists.

He visited Tuskegee and Birmingham in Alabama and troubled Little Rock in Arkansas, everywhere feeling the same uncanny connection to the land that said to him, in some way, that he had finally come home, as well as realizing that little in his own experience had prepared him for what he would see in the South. In the remarkable essay "Nobody Knows My Name," he wrote of looking into the eyes of an old black man as he, Baldwin, prepared to board the first segregated bus he had ever been made to ride in his life: "And it was, perhaps, because I was getting on a segregated bus, and wondering how Negroes had borne this and other indignities for so long, that this man so struck me. He seemed to know what I was feeling. His eyes seemed to say that what I was feeling he had been feeling, at much higher pressure, all his life. But my eyes would never see the hell his eyes had seen. And this hell was, simply, that he had never in his life owned anything, not his wife, not his house, not his child, which could not, at any instant, be taken from him by the power of white people." In the South, Baldwin also discovered that he had never known true terror, but that, paradoxically, at this point in the region's history, terror was producing not defeat and submission in southern blacks but something quite different: a passion, almost religious in its power, uniting black men and women as a single community. "I doubt that I really knew much about terror before I went south," Baldwin would write in *No Name in the Street,* a reminiscence of his civil rights years published in 1972, many years after his first trip to the South. "This terror can produce its own antidote: an overwhelming pride and rage, so that, whether or not one is ready to die, one gives every appearance of being willing to die."

In "Nobody Knows My Name," Baldwin proposed that the white South's resistance to desegregation and to the legitimate aspirations of black citizens had as much to do with sexual guilt as it did with political, social, and economic power. Color, as Baldwin would put it in "Down at the Cross," "is not a human and personal reality; it is a political one," an essentially fictional distinction created to maintain social, economic, and political privilege, and segregation, as the legal and social system erected to enforce these privileges, was on a human level a logical absurdity. The South had, in one significant way, in fact been integrated long ago, Baldwin argued; "integrated in the womb," as he often put it. "Negroes and whites in this country are related to each other," he told Studs Terkel in 1961. "Half of the black families in the South are related, you know, to the judges and the lawyers and the white families of the South." In fact, a pioneering study done by anthropologist Melville Herskovits earlier in the century had estimated that upwards of 70 percent of American blacks had white ancestors. Frederick Douglass and Booker T. Washington were just two prominent African Americans, born in slavery, known to have been fathered by their white master; the founding fathers Thomas Jefferson, Patrick Henry, and Alexander Hamilton are all believed to have fathered children with slave women, and Hamilton was even reputed to have had some black blood.

Blacks in the United States are actually "every color under heaven," Baldwin observed in 1970. "Whatever he or anyone else may wish to believe," Baldwin wrote in "Nobody Knows My Name," a black man knows "that his ancestors are both white and black"; as the embodiment of their sexual guilt and sexual transgressions, "white men, flesh of his flesh, hate him for that very reason." In the same essay, a black man in Alabama tells Baldwin that "integration has always worked very well in the South, after the sun goes down"; another black observed that "it's not miscegenation [sexual relations, prohibited under Southern custom and law, between a white and a black] unless a black man is involved." (Years later, in his last original work, *The Evidence of Things Not Seen,* Baldwin quoted an old black woman in Alabama as saying, "White people don't hate Black people—if they did, we'd all be Black.")

For decades, the conventional justification for lynching given by white southerners had been sexual offenses against white women by black men. Whites defined such sexual offenses very broadly; just two

Mamie Bradley (center) of Chicago, Illinois, weeps over the coffin containing the body of her 14-year-old son, Emmett Till, who was lynched in Mississippi while on a summertime visit to a relative for supposedly impertinent behavior toward a white woman. Though the killers later confessed their misdeeds to a journalist, an all-white jury acquitted them. The killing and its aftermath inspired Baldwin's play *Blues for Mr. Charlie.*

years before Baldwin's first trip to the South, in Money, Mississippi, a 14-year-old black child, Emmett Till, had been beaten, shot in the head, mutilated, and disposed of in the Tallahatchee River by two white men for the crime of saying "Bye, babe" to the white woman who served him in a general store. But, Baldwin perceptively argued in "Nobody Knows My Name," what was really at play in such acts was white guilt about their own sexual attraction to blacks, and guilt about the way in which their exercise of power over blacks had enabled them to exercise their lust without consequence. That guilt was written "somewhere" where it could be seen "all the time": in "the eyes of the black man." To whites, blacks were therefore a living reminder of truths about themselves that they could not bring themselves to face—truths about the real nature of American history, about their own sexuality, morality, and identity, and ultimately about America's national character.

Though he would steadfastly resist acknowledging the role of spokesman—"I'm still trying to speak just for me, not for 20 million people," he told journalist and critic Nat Hentoff in 1963—for the next several years Baldwin would devote much of his time and energy to civil rights. He recognized that this took a toll on his artistic life, admitting that he was "stealing from the artist," as he told an interviewer in 1963, to pay for the success of the movement, but his ideas about the political responsibility of the writer had changed somewhat since the years of his debates with Richard Wright. Then, Wright had accused him of an irresponsible adherence to a philosophy of "art for art's sake," with Wright proclaiming that "all literature is protest." Over time, Baldwin would come to believe that writing "was political, whether one liked it or not, because if one is doing anything at all [in writing], one is trying to change the consciousness of other people"—a political act in itself, akin to that in which the civil rights demonstrators in the South were engaged.

Because of his essays and activism, Baldwin was invariably associated in the public mind with the cause of civil rights, but he was never really a leader of the movement. Instead, he used his growing fame and oratorical ability to focus public attention on the movement and its goals, giving a seemingly endless string of speeches in the North and

South to raise money for such groups as the NAACP, SNCC, and the Southern Christian Leadership Council (SCLC). Though Baldwin had left the church long ago, the moral fervor of his years as a young minister remained with him, and audiences invariably found the small, frail man with the gap-toothed smile and the penetrating, protruding eyes charismatic and inspirational.

The leadership of the civil rights movement was often more ambivalent about Baldwin's participation. Genuinely grateful for the energy and devotion Baldwin brought to his role—which was, as movement activist Bayard Rustin described it, "to use his fame to raise funds and make friends and bring us media publicity"—the movement leadership, especially the older and more conservative ministers from the SCLC, were nonetheless made uneasy by Baldwin's homosexuality, fearing that it could be used, as was knowledge of Martin Luther King's numerous extramarital affairs, to discredit the movement. Indeed, Baldwin's involvement in the movement made him, like King, the subject of near-constant FBI attention, in the form of phone taps and other surveillance, much of it, as was also the case with King, focusing on his personal life. As Baldwin was so open about his sexual preferences, any government attempt at blackmailing him into silence, as was tried with King, would most likely have met with failure, but the possibility of disclosures worried King and his advisers nonetheless. (In King's case, he was subjected to constant wiretapping, bugging of rooms where he was staying, and other surveillance by the FBI, with the implicit threat that the bureau would use such information to destroy him; on one occasion the FBI, by way of a forged letter, threatened to make public tapes of King engaging in sex with a woman other than his wife unless, the letter strongly implied, he committed suicide.) As a result, Baldwin was kept at something of a distance by civil rights leaders. In private conversation (bugged by the FBI), King was heard to say that although Baldwin was considered by the press to be a spokesman for black Americans, he was not a civil rights leader and that he was in fact more qualified to "lead a homosexual movement than a civil rights movement." And at the high point of the movement, the famous March on Washington on August 28, 1963, Baldwin was excluded, to his anger, from the roster of speakers who addressed the huge crowd of 250,000.

Despite his frenetic lifestyle, with its eternal round of personal appearances, demonstrations, fund-raisers, radio and televison interviews—he likened himself to a jazz musician on an endless tour of one-nighters—Baldwin was able to complete a sizable body of significant work during the late 1950s and early 1960s. Though usually on the move, he now had a home base of sorts to work from, a small rented apartment on Horatio Street in Greenwich Village. There, and at various refuges outside the city (usually the homes of friends) to which he periodically fled to escape the social whirl that made writing difficult, he devoted himself, as time and his increasing fondness for socializing and nightlife allowed, to a number of projects, including a stage adaptation of *Giovanni's Room* for the renowned Actor's Studio; various magazine assignments and essays that would be collected in *Nobody Knows My Name*; short stories, including one of his most well-known, "This Morning, This Evening, So Soon"; and most important, the ambitious novel of interracial and bisexual love that would eventually appear under the title *Another Country*.

Nobody Knows My Name was published in 1961 to rapturous reviews, great public acclaim, and considerable commercial success that made Baldwin unquestionably the best-known and most important black writer in America, if not simply the most important American writer. It stayed on the nonfiction best-seller lists for six months, virtually unheard of for a collection of essays, and won numerous citations as one of the most important volumes of the year. Reviewers called the book "bright and alive" and "brilliant and masterly," and its author "among the most penetrating and perceptive of American thinkers."

Where, in a general sense, *Notes of a Native Son,* in its broad range of subject matter, was devoted to the ways in which America makes exiles of all its black citizens by imparting again and again the message that their individual existence is of meaningless consequence to the real life of the nation, *Nobody Knows My Name,* which begins with Baldwin's discussion of the reasons why it became necessary for him to return to the United States, examines what it means for a black to be an American, with the implication that at stake in the answer to this question is nothing less than the true national identity.

"The question of color," writes Baldwin in the collection's introduction, "especially in this country, operates to hide the graver questions of the self"; if the nation as a whole is ever to answer that graver question and experience the revelation that Baldwin assigns as the title of his first essay in the book—The Discovery of What It Means To Be an American—"it must re-examine itself and discover what it really means by freedom." For all the hysteria of white southerners over maintaining segregation, Baldwin argues over the course of 13 essays, which range in ostensible subject matter from the work of Richard Wright, William Faulkner, and André Gide to public housing projects in Harlem, his own time in the South, and even to the films of the Swedish director Ingmar Bergman, there never has been and never can be a true separation of the races, who are tied together by history, blood, and common interest: the future of the country is the future of both. "My own experience proves to me," a still hopeful Baldwin wrote in his introduction, "that the connection between American whites and blacks is far deeper and more passionate than any of us like to think."

If the constant activity surrounding Baldwin had been disruptive before, the success of *Nobody Knows My Name* made the demands on his time truly maddening. His civil rights commitments intensified, requests for interviews increased, and he found it ever more difficult to resist socializing, spending many nights in restaurants and bars with a large entourage, often drinking heavily. Solitude, a painful necessity for any writer, became increasingly hard to come by. "People always seemed to know where I was hiding my typewriter," he said. "They were always dropping by at all times of the day and night. . . . I had to get away." He tried the Westchester County home of his editor at Dial Press, but people found him, and the party began anew.

He tried Paris, but he had too many friends there, old and new, and the urge to socialize was too strong. So he continued moving, all the way to Istanbul, Turkey, where he had been invited to visit by the young Turkish actor, Engin Cezzar, who had played the Italian bartender in the Actor's Studio production of *Giovanni's Room*. In this

Baldwin with a couple of young friends in Istanbul, where he finished his third novel, *Another Country.* The Turkish city served him intermittently as a refuge from the increasing demands on his time and energy that his growing fame inspired.

exotic location, in a rented apartment on a hill overlooking the Bosporus, he finished in several months—on December 10, 1961—the novel on which he had been working for six years.

Though he was reasonably confident about the artistic achievement of his new work—"my best novel so far . . . harder and more challenging

96

than anything I've done"—and knew that Dial Press was clamoring for the book, Baldwin was somewhat apprehensive regarding the public's response to his novel, for *Another Country* is an unsparing and unforgiving look at racial and sexual relations in the United States, in which no one—black, white, male, female—gets off easily. Set primarily in the

97

bohemian Greenwich Village of the late 1950s, the novel nevertheless encompasses much of Baldwin's life experience, from the harsher streets of Harlem to the American expatriate colony in France. In *Another Country,* Baldwin wrote about gay love and straight love and bisexual love just as he had done before, but this time he mixed all five of his major characters—Rufus Scott, jazz drummer and suicide, and his sister Ida, an aspiring jazz singer; her lover Vivaldo Moore, an unpublished novelist; his and Rufus's lover Eric, an actor on the verge of stardom; and Eric's lover Cass, wife of Richard Silenski, a commercially successful but not very talented novelist—into a complex configuration of interactions that encompass the full range of ways any two people can be together: a kind, on the personal level, of complete social and sexual integration.

Baldwin uses this complicated construction to make a deceptively simple point—love is our only salvation and the race or gender of whom you love simply does not matter—but the fate of his characters proves how difficult and genuinely painful any kind of love can be. To genuinely love, Baldwin repeatedly affirms in his novels and essays, one must face the truth about oneself, and if each of the major characters in *Another Country*—except perhaps for Rufus, who is destroyed—gains a profounder understanding of himself or herself as a result of the relationships charted in this essentially plotless novel, that knowledge comes at the cost of great personal pain and suffering.

Yet though the novel offers little real hope that any of the lovers have a future together, their efforts to connect have not been in vain. By love, Baldwin would write the following year in "Down at the Cross," he meant "a state of being, or a state of grace—not in the infantile American sense of being made happy but in the tough and universal sense of quest and daring and growth." The fictional characters of *Another Country* embody that notion; though they suffer much, they also move much closer toward that point, as Baldwin describes it in "Down at the Cross," where "one eventually ceases to be controlled by a fear of what life can bring." And it is at that point, Baldwin goes on to say, that one is able to stop hating and stop fearing. Though the novel focuses relentlessly on the personal (none of Baldwin's characters takes part in a demonstration, for example, or discusses a social issue on any terms other than how it relates to them personally), it is no less concerned with the state of national affairs than Baldwin's essays. Freedom is personal, Baldwin had written in "Nobody Knows My Name"; it is "a complex, difficult—and private—thing." It "demands of everyone who loves this country a hard look at himself, for the greatest achievements must begin somewhere, and they always begin with the person." The characters in Baldwin's novel have met that demand and taken that hard look, with the implication being that if everyone were to do so, we would "discover" (Baldwin's word, in several interviews; elsewhere, and more famously, he used "achieve") another country.

Baldwin need not have worried about the critical and commercial reception that would greet *Another Country*. Though some critics would damn the book as "mediocre" and a "failure," even as "pornography," others would call it a "shattering experience" and "one of the most powerful novels of our time." Perhaps the most meaningful praise came from Edmund Wilson, writing in the *New Yorker*: "Not only [is Baldwin] one of the best Negro writers we have ever had in this country, he is one of the best writers." Despite being banned in New Orleans, Louisiana, as "obscene," *Another Country* topped the hard-cover national best-seller lists for weeks at a time in 1962. When the paperback was released in 1963, it became the second largest-selling book of the year.

Five months after the June 1962 publication of *Another Country,* Baldwin weighed in, in the form of an essay in the the *New Yorker* entitled "Letter from a Region in My Mind" and later published in the book *The Fire Next Time* as "Down at the Cross," with a warning to his nation about the likely future consequences of its inability or unwillingness to address its racial problems.

While Martin Luther King's nonviolence crusade continued to gather strength in the South, a different sort of movement, with very different philosophies and goals, was winning adherents among blacks in the cities of the North. The Nation of Islam, as it was officially known (its followers were commonly referred to as Black Muslims), had its origins in the United States in the 1930s. Its leaders, most notable among them Elijah Muhammad, combined a message of black pride and racial separatism with the tenets of traditional Islam. Many Black Muslims, such as the charismatic Malcolm X, who by the early 1960s had become the movement's best-known spokesman and Elijah

Baldwin in early 1963, around the time that *The Fire Next Time* was published. "[Blacks and whites] cannot separate," Baldwin told an interviewer in 1970. "The tragedy of the white people is that they always thought they could, and the result of that thinking has been social chaos, which will get worse yet."

Muhammad's likely successor, had come to the religion in jail, where the Nation of Islam, with its emphasis on self-respect and self-discipline and its prohibition of the use of drugs, alcohol, or tobacco, had enjoyed great success at rehabilitation. By the early 1960s, the Nation of Islam's philosophy of black separatism and economic self-sufficiency, as opposed to integration; of self-defense, as opposed to nonviolence; and of black superiority, as opposed to King's Christian love—the Black Muslims taught that all whites were evil "devils"—had won it a wide following in the North, especially in the black ghettos of such cities as Detroit, Chicago, and New York, and a fearsome reputation with whites as an organization of militant, probably violent, extremists.

"Down at the Cross" was born from an August 1961 visit that Baldwin made to Elijah Muhammad at the Nation of Islam's Chicago headquarters. The visit sparked, in well-wrought, prophetic prose, a long contemplation—generally considered Baldwin's masterpiece—of his own past, specifically the appeal that religion had held for him at the time of his own coming of age, and the reasons for, and potential consequences of, the appeal that the Black Muslims held for a new generation of black youth. As with so much of his work, the moral weight of the piece centered on his ongoing, lifelong struggle to balance the "tension in me between love and power, between pain and rage," to overcome hatred and bitterness while steadfastly opposing the injustice from which they spring. The Black Muslims were not altogether new to him; he had heard their message proclaimed by orators from soapboxes on the corners of Harlem streets since his youth, and in its essence their rhetoric was not all that different from his father's. There was, he found, much to admire about the Black Muslims—their discipline and pride, their dignity—and Baldwin acknowledged that there was truth in Malcolm X's statement that "the cry of violence . . . is raised only when black men indicate that they will fight for *their* rights." To Baldwin, the appeal of the Black Muslims, with their promise to build a separate black nation and their theological certainty that the historical epoch of white rule was coming to an imminent end, was understandable—"things are as bad as the Muslims say they are," he wrote; "in fact, they are worse"—but their message was unacceptable. It was, finally, racist, and the challenge was to get past racism. He had, he wrote, to "oppose any attempt that Negroes may make to do to others what has been done to them," for "that road leads" to a "spiritual wasteland" and ignores the lesson made so glaringly evident by the appalling spectacle of those racist whites of the South driven to extremes in the defense of segregation: "Whoever debases others is debasing himself." Though all blacks had good reason to wonder, as Baldwin put it, "do I really want to be integrated into a burning house," he was to conclude that the only future for American blacks was as Americans, just as the only future for America was to extend the full measure of freedom promised all its citizens to blacks.

"In order to change a situation one has first to see it for what it is: in the present case, to accept the fact, whatever one does with it thereafter, that the Negro has been formed by this nation, for better or for worse, and does not belong to any other—not to Africa, and certainly not to Islam," wrote Baldwin, who had long since determined that the one immutable aspect of his identity was that he was an American. Separatism is a "dream," he reiterated in an interview several years later; "that's like talking about the separation of a family," which did not excuse white America from facing the truth and living up to its responsibilities. "[The black] is the key figure in the country," Baldwin wrote in "Down at the Cross," and "the American future is precisely as bright or as dark as his." A "bill" was coming due, warned Baldwin, for the country's long history of racial injustice, and he feared that his fellow citizens would be unwilling to pay it, and feared even more the consequences of that delinquency. "What will happen to all that beauty, then?" he asks, referring to the fact that "black people, though I am aware that some of us, black and white, do not know it yet, are very beautiful."

The challenge facing Americans, more pressing than ever at that particular historical moment, according to Baldwin, was to create a society that recognized that "the value placed on the color of the skin is always and everywhere and forever a delusion." That challenge, he recognized, might well be impossible, but "American Negro history," an endured and surmounted past "of rope, fire, torture, castration, infanticide, rape; death and humiliation; fear by day and night, fear as deep as the marrow of the bone . . . testifies to nothing less than the perpetual achievement of the impossible." Failure would mean the exaction of "historical vengeance, a cosmic vengeance, based on the law that we recognize when we say 'Whatever goes up must come down.'" He concluded by quoting the words of a black spiritual to convey an apocalyptic warning: "If we—and now I mean the relatively conscious whites and the relatively conscious blacks, who must, like lovers, insist on, or create, the consciousness of the others—do not falter in our duty now, we may be able, handful that we are, to end the racial nightmare, and achieve our country, and change the history of the world. If we do not now dare everything, the fulfillment of that prophecy, re-created from the Bible in song by a slave, is upon us: *God gave Noah the rainbow sign, No more water, the fire next time!*"

CHAPTER SEVEN

WHAT WILL HAPPEN TO ALL THAT BEAUTY?

Baldwin's essay appeared in the November 17, 1962, issue of the *New Yorker*. The magazine was renowned, as few such journals have been, for the consistent excellence of its writing, but according to its legendary longtime editor, William Shawn, Baldwin's piece was "one of only two or three things that caused a sensation during my time at the magazine." The magazine quickly sold out, and to Baldwin's surprise, Dial Press wanted to publish the essay on its own as *The Fire Next Time*. (He added a brief prefatory piece in the form of a letter to his nephew, "My Dungeon Shook," to flesh out the volume.) The hardcover book rocketed to the top of the best-seller lists and stayed there for nearly a year, and the paperback edition, for which Baldwin received the then princely sum of $65,000, did nearly as well. *Time* magazine put Baldwin on its cover and profiled the author—in the national affairs, not the

Baldwin in his New York City apartment in 1963. Above him on the wall are photographs of Beauford Delaney. "Talent is insignificant, " he once said. "Beyond talent lie all the usual words: discipline, love, luck, but, most of all, endurance."

105

literature, section. According to *Time,* "In the United States today there is not another writer, black or white, who expresses with such poignancy and abrasiveness the dark realities of the racial ferment in North and South." A profile in *Esquire* magazine noted that "rarely has any American writer had so much public renown." More meaningful was the observation of the eminent literary critic Lionel Trilling: "There is probably no literary career in America that matches James Baldwin's in the degree of interest it commands."

Despite his protests that he remained first and foremost an artist, Baldwin was clearly being pegged as a spokesman—and as a celebrity.

Baldwin arrives at Kennedy Airport in New York City from Paris in 1965. In the early 1960s, newspapers and magazines seemed to follow every move made by the celebrated author.

When he made a tour of speaking engagements in the South, including a visit to Oxford, Mississippi, to lend moral support to James Meredith, a black man whose attempt to enroll at the previously all-white University of Mississippi in the fall of 1962 provoked rioting and the need for President John F. Kennedy to send 20,000 federal troops to Oxford to keep the peace and ensure his safety, *Life* magazine sent along a reporter to cover his every move. Back in New York, the magazine's writer noted, "it is a sign of considerable chic to know James Baldwin well enough to refer to him as Jimmy." Many claimed that privilege; at home Baldwin's life seemed to be a nonstop whirlwind of party going and restaurant- and barhopping, always with a large group of friends, with most nights not ending until near dawn, when the inevitable after-hours celebration at his Village apartment wound down. Baldwin, the *Life* reporter wrote, "was the monarch of the literary jungle."

The Oxford crisis had shocked the Kennedy administration, which, until the violence on the campus of "Ole Miss," had failed to realize how deeply entrenched the notion of white superiority and segregation was in white southern culture. The violence in Mississippi moved President Kennedy to propose a civil rights bill to Congress in February 1963, but movement leaders and black citizens throughout the United States, while generally acknowledging that the Kennedy administration had done more than any previous one for the cause of civil rights, continued to believe that the federal government could make an even more meaningful commitment to racial equality. Their frustration mounted, as did the astonishment of the Kennedy administration and of many more sympathetic whites, when, in May 1963, police in Birmingham, Alabama, blasted black schoolchildren peacefully protesting segregation in that city with water from high-pressure fire hoses and unleashed attack dogs on them.

Seeking a black perspective on the situation, Robert Kennedy, attorney general in his brother's administration and the government official entrusted by the president with responsibility for civil rights, asked Baldwin to assemble a group of black leaders and meet with him at his family's apartment in New York City on May 24, 1963, to discuss racial issues, particularly the problems of the northern ghettos. Robert

Firemen in Birmingham, Alabama, blast protesting black schoolchildren with water from fire hoses. The frightening image of black children being knocked off their feet by the stream from special high-pressure hoses and set upon by police dogs served for many Americans as the ultimate demonstration of the moral bankruptcy of the segregationists' position.

Kennedy and Baldwin had met the previous year, at a White House dinner for Nobel prizewinners to which the author had been invited, and had gotten along well; Kennedy assumed that Baldwin, because of his Harlem background, might have insight into the racial problems of the North.

Baldwin brought with him an extraordinary array of prominent black Americans: Kenneth Clark, educator and psychologist; Edwin Berry, director of the Chicago Urban League; Clarence Jones, one of Martin Luther King's attorneys; Lorraine Hansberry, the noted playwright; Lena Horne, singer and actress; Harry Belafonte, singer and actor; and Jerome Smith, a young black activist who had been badly beaten for taking part in civil rights protests in the South. Significantly, though all of these individuals had, to varying degrees, lent their support to the civil rights movement, none of them was truly a leader of it. The meeting had been arranged at extremely short notice; though King was asked to attend, he was unable to do so and asked Clark to represent him. Several of the black participants wondered nonetheless why Kennedy, if he was sincerely interested in civil rights issues, had not invited more of the actual leaders of the movement to meet with him.

Kennedy brought with him Burke Marshall, one of his top aides, for the encounter, which Clark would later describe as "the most intense, traumatic meeting in which I've ever taken part . . . the most unrestrained interchange among adults, head-to-head, no holds barred . . . *the* most dramatic experience I have ever had." (The best and most complete account of the meeting is in Arthur Schlesinger's biography, *Robert Kennedy and His Times*.) Kennedy was apparently expecting a sober, reasoned discussion of policy and issues, with statistical analyses and concrete proposals, but Baldwin and most of his company had another purpose in mind: to bear witness to what it felt like to be a black in America at that time, to attempt to impress upon the attorney general the depth of the frustration and emotion blacks were feeling at white America's resistance to their pleas for justice.

It was a message that Kennedy was not immediately prepared to hear. Smith, still bearing visible welts and scars from his treatment in the South, began by stammering that the very need for having such a meeting made him sick. The young freedom rider meant that injustice and inequality of the kind he had risked his life to protest had no place in American society, that it was long past time that the government did something to end them, but Kennedy interpreted the words as a personal attack. The attorney general only grew more defensive when Smith, a dedicated pacifist, stated that he (and by implication, many blacks like him) was rapidly reaching the point where he could no longer commit himself to nonviolence. "When I pull the trigger," Smith said, "kiss it good-bye." Here was Baldwin's prediction of the fire next time embodied in one who had been on the front lines, who had suffered physically as a result of his commitment to nonviolence but could no longer pledge himself to a peaceful solution to America's racial ills. In response to a question from Baldwin, Smith went on to say to the appalled Kennedy that he would "never! never! never!" fight for his country.

Stunned by Smith's vehemence and by his evocation of a level of emotion and experience so foreign to his own, Kennedy responded as if under attack, criticizing the young activist for his lack of patriotism, attempting to defend the administration's commitment to civil rights, and seeking to steer the conversation toward specific policy recommendations, only to be shouted down in what Clark afterward described as "really one of the most violent, emotional verbal assaults . . . that I had ever witnessed before or since." The other blacks in the room sprang to Smith's defense. What Smith had to say, they sought to impress upon the attorney general, was the truth about how blacks in the United States felt, a truth more meaningful, more real than any statistical chart or policy proposal—a truth that whites needed to understand before any real change could occur. "This boy [Smith]," Lena Horne remembered afterward, "just put it like it was. He communicated the plain, basic suffering of being a Negro." Lorraine Hansberry implored Kennedy to truly hear what Smith was saying and again invoked the fire next time, warning that blacks could not be expected to remain nonviolent: "Look, if *you* can't understand what this young man is saying, then we are without any hope at all because you and your brother are representatives of the best that a white American can offer; and if *you* are insensitive to this then there's no alternative except our going in the streets . . . chaos." Baldwin suggested that as a powerful symbolic gesture, President Kennedy personally escort to classes the two black students then attempting, over the opposition of Governor George Wallace and a large percentage of the state's white population, to integrate the University of Alabama. Kennedy rejected the idea as, in Schlesinger's words, "theatrical posturing."

And so the discussion continued, with Baldwin's group growing ever more impassioned and Kennedy, in Clark's words, first "purple" with rage, then increasingly more "silent and tense," until after three wearying hours the meeting broke up. Both parties left with a feeling of despair, afraid that what had just been revealed was that the gap between the experiences and understandings of whites and blacks was just too wide to be bridged, even by the most well-meaning of potential allies. Baldwin believed that Kennedy simply "didn't understand what we were trying to tell him . . . didn't understand our urgency," while Clark felt "that the whole thing was hopeless; that there was no chance that

Baldwin drinks to the opening-night success of his play *Blues for Mr. Charlie* with the play's female lead, Diana Sands, and its director, Burgess Meredith.

Martin Luther King (left) and Malcolm X (right) shake hands during a meeting in Washington, D.C., on March 26, 1964, to discuss strategy regarding President Lyndon Johnson's civil rights bill. Though the two black leaders differed greatly on tactics and philosophy, Baldwin believed that both of their messages needed to be heard if America was to cure its racial ills, and their murders left him devastated

[Kennedy] heard anything that we said. . . . [He] was not unimpressive. He didn't minimize or condescend. But he just didn't seem to get it." For his part, Kennedy felt that Baldwin's delegation had been uninterested in a genuine dialogue, uninterested in concrete proposals. "They seemed possessed," Kennedy told Schlesinger. "They reacted as a unit. It was impossible to make contact with them." But, said Clark, his delegation had been "shocked that [Kennedy] was shocked" at the passion of their presentation. Evidence that their feelings were not unique to themselves was available all around the country; the meeting took place near the midpoint of a 10-week period following the Birmingham demonstrations in which it was estimated that there were 758 separate civil rights protests, resulting in the arrest of 14,733 civil rights activists, in 158 different American cities.

Though in the wake of their famous meeting Baldwin would tell a *New York Times* interviewer that "despair is a sin," and Kennedy would begin a process of personal growth—stimulated, in large part, in the opinion of both Schlesinger and Belafonte, by their bitter debate—that left little doubt that the attorney general was one of the "relatively conscious whites" in whom Baldwin had placed some degree of hope, future events would seem to justify the overriding sense of pessimism with which its participants left the encounter. The most immediate of these events was the mid-June assassination of NAACP leader Medgar Evers in Jackson, Mississippi, on the same night that President Kennedy went on television to announce his commitment to civil rights as a "moral issue."

He had no way of knowing it, of course, but Baldwin had already reached the pinnacle of his influence, both as an artist and as an activist and spokesman. In August 1963, the March on Washington gave civil rights supporters reason for optimism, but Baldwin himself was hurt by his exclusion from the roster of speakers, and the bombing of a black church in Birmingham fewer than three weeks later, in which four black children were killed, reconfirmed the distance that blacks still had to travel, as did Baldwin's unproductive trip to Selma in early October. Almost six weeks later, on November 22, John Kennedy was murdered in Dallas, Texas. The president's death was "a tremendous loss," Baldwin told reporters. "You could argue with him. He could hear. He began to see. There was no reason for him, a Boston millionaire's son, to know more about blacks than anybody else. But he could listen."

Political commitments and the temptations of celebrity continued to eat away at Baldwin's time to write, but he did manage to complete a play based on the tragic murder of Emmett Till, *Blues for Mr. Charlie*, written, he said, on buses and airplanes and in gas stations, "all sorts of places." Produced by Lee Strasberg, the legendary founder of the Actor's Studio, directed by Burgess Meredith, and starring Rip Torn, the play opened on Broadway in late April 1964 and ran for a respectable four months. Baldwin was nevertheless somewhat disappointed by the public's response, fearing that potential playgoers had been put off by persistent criticism that the play was less drama than polemic, an essentially anti-white diatribe that revealed his growing despair over the state of black-white relations in the United States. The play's production was associated with an unpleasant personal experience as well: Lucien Happersberger, who had divorced his wife and moved to the United States to act as Baldwin's manager, fell in love with and then married the beautiful female lead in the play, the young black actress Diana Sands. Baldwin apparently regarded the marriage as a betrayal; according to a friend quoted by Campbell, news of the union prompted Baldwin to break furniture in the huge new apartment he had bought on West End Avenue.

Those who knew Baldwin best detected a certain restlessness and sadness in him. Always in the company, it seemed, of celebrity friends, members of his family, or one of a long succession of young male companions (none of whom, to this date, has cared to speak publicly about their life with Baldwin), he seemed nonetheless lonely and afraid to be by himself. Genuinely proud of his fame—"I'm probably the most photographed writer in the world," he remarked with wonder at one point—he yet chafed at the incongruities of his position. Fame, he observed, did not make it any more likely that a taxi driver would stop his cab, once he got close enough to recognize that his prospective fare was a black man, and when he decided to buy a house on West 71st Street (where many members of his family would live with him at different times), Lucien had to act as a front, for real estate agents were reluctant to show or sell to blacks. Yet his books, several critics pointed out, were read more by whites than by blacks, and he worried that he might be, as he later put it, nothing more than "the Great Black Hope of the Great White Father"; he began to say that he hoped blacks would respond to his work the same way they did to the music of the pianist and vocalist Ray Charles or the trumpeter Miles Davis, the most popular and important black musicians of the day. As did King, he came under increased criticism from more militant black leaders and activists,

Baldwin enjoys a smoke from a hookah at an outdoor restaurant in Istanbul. "The principal reason that I now find myself in Istanbul," Baldwin told an interviewer in 1967, "is that I am a writer, and I find it easier to write here than I do elsewhere."

particularly Malcolm X, for his "accommodationist" viewpoints, yet when he made his message more strident and less forgiving, as in *Blues for Mr. Charlie* and in the discussion he orchestrated with Robert Kennedy, whites seemed to stop listening.

He resolved his confusion as he had done in the past: by leaving the United States. He wandered, sometimes in the company of friends and family members, to Paris and London and finally to Istanbul (with frequent return trips to the United States), in search, he said, of a quiet place where people would leave him alone and he could write. A collection of eight short stories, *Going to Meet the Man,* which he dedicated to Beauford Delaney, appeared in 1965, but the reviews were not encouraging: respectful, generally, but rarely enthusiastic. Some of the stories—notably "Sonny's Blues," about the relationship between two brothers, one of them a troubled yet talented jazz pianist; and "This Morning, This Evening, So Soon," about an expatriate black American singer in Europe—were superb, but none of them, with the exception of the title piece, was new, and after *Another Country* and *The Fire Next Time* critics expected Baldwin to break new ground every time out. Baldwin himself believed that the critics were responding to what they regarded as an increasingly militant attitude on his part toward white people. "The general opinion seems to be I was a nice sweet cat with talent when I was twenty but now I'm bitter and it's had a terrible effect on my work," he told Weatherby.

If he had grown more pessimistic, less forgiving, it was not without reason. On February 21, 1965, Malcolm X had been shot and killed while speaking at the Audubon Ballroom in Harlem. Without tempering his criticism of racism in the slightest, Malcolm, after making a pilgrimage to Mecca, the holy city of Islam, had renounced his belief that all whites were evil, having "learned the hard way" that "brotherhood" was the "only thing that [could] save this country," and Baldwin had come to admire him a great deal. After Malcolm unexpectedly showed up at a Baldwin lecture one day, seating himself in the front row, the two men had become friends, with Baldwin recognizing that beneath the fiery, even frightening, rhetoric—"I was a little afraid of him, as was everyone else," he said of their early encounters—Malcolm "was one of the gentlest people I have ever met." Baldwin would continue to denounce the Nation of Islam as racist, but Malcolm, who had broken with the group after denunciating Elijah Muhammad's sexual misconduct, was something different, as Baldwin would explain in *No Name in the Street*: "His intelligence was more complex than that; furthermore, if he had been a racist, not many in this racist country would have considered him dangerous. . . . What made him unfamiliar and dangerous was not his hatred for white people, but his love for blacks, his apprehension of the horror of the black condition . . . and his determination so to work on their hearts and minds that they would be enabled to see their condition and change it themselves." More than King, Malcolm appealed to the young blacks of the North and the more militant elements of the civil rights movement—he continued to denounce King's policy of nonviolence—but Baldwin felt that both men were necessary to the success of the movement.

Eldridge Cleaver, minister of information of the Black Panther party, stands in front of the bullet-riddled headquarters of the party in Oakland, California, on September 11, 1968, following a drive-by shooting by Oakland policemen. At left in the headquarters' window is a picture of Huey P. Newton, the party's chairman.

News of Malcolm's murder reached Baldwin while he was in London, and he reacted, predictably, with great emotion. The killers were members of the Nation of Islam, which had been threatening Malcolm since their break, but Baldwin's response was that the identity of the killer was not as important as the legacy of racial hatred that created the climate in which such a deed was possible. "Whatever hand pulled the trigger did not buy the bullet," he told the press in London. "That bullet was forged in the crucible of the West, that death was dictated by the most successful conspiracy in the history of the world, and its name is white supremacy." The press reported that he had accused innocent people of Malcolm's murder, and his comments were chalked up as one more supposed example of his growing extremism.

But to the young and increasingly militant leaders of the civil rights movement—those, such as Stokely Carmichael, the new head of SNCC, who were preaching the virtue of "black power," and the leather-clad members of the Black Panther party, the swaggering, self-proclaimed "sons of Malcolm," with their rifles and berets—he was still too moderate, increasingly irrelevant, a relic. Though Baldwin lent public support to the Black Panther party, which proclaimed that the behavior of white society constituted a war against blacks, echoed the Chinese leader Mao Zedong's belief that all political power comes from the barrel of a gun, and recommended that blacks arm themselves against police oppression, the Panthers, especially their Minister of Information, Eldridge Cleaver, did not necessarily return his regard. In an essay entitled "Notes on a Native Son," which appeared first in *Ramparts* magazine and then in his 1968 best-selling book *Soul on Ice,* Cleaver criticized Baldwin's work as the literary counterpart of King's self-defeating, needlessly accommodationist policies and proclaimed the writer's homosexuality the equivalent of a "racial death-wish." He accused Baldwin of hating himself and other black people, called him "shameful," "fawning," and "womanish," and said that he cowered before "real men." Baldwin's response was measured—"all that toy soldier has done is call me gay," he told Weatherby, and in *No Name in the Street* he wrote of his general admiration for *Soul on Ice* and characterized Cleaver as "valuable and rare"—but the criticism rankled

"Since Martin's death in Memphis and that tremendous day in Atlanta [King's funeral], something has altered in me, something has gone away," Baldwin wrote in *No Name in the Street.*

nonetheless. Fewer than five years after he had been lionized as the activist literary voice of black America, Baldwin was being dismissed by a younger generation.

Seemingly out of step politically, Baldwin also found that his work continued to be less well received than in the past. More than a decade after he had written it, *The Amen Corner* was finally produced on Broadway, but it opened to poor reviews and played only a short run. In June 1968, Dial published his new novel, *Tell Me How Long the Train's Been Gone,* completed somehow amidst the hectic whirlwind of his private life and public commitments. The story of Leo Proudhammer, a successful black bisexual actor from a poor background, the novel was intended by Baldwin to be an examination of the wages of success, an exploration of "the star or celebrity game" in which he found himself enmeshed. Despite a review in *Commentary* that called the book a "masterpiece," the critics in general were savage. The book was dismissed either as self-involved and irrelevant or as polemical and propagandistic, with one-dimensional characters and a surprisingly leaden style.

Baldwin tended to attribute the reviews to political bias—near the end of the novel, a young black militant named Black Christopher proclaims "we need guns"—but it was clear that a certain spirit had gone out of his writing; his editors at Dial were greatly surprised when he expressed little interest in discussing proposed changes to the manuscript and finally told them to go ahead and do whatever they wanted. By the time the book came out, Baldwin was able to care very little at all about its reception—though the frustration and rage embodied by Black Christopher seemed to him more understandable than ever—for he was attempting to deal with the anguish caused him by the assassination, two months earlier, of Martin Luther King. When the tragic news reached him in Palm Springs, California, where he was engaged in an ultimately unsuccessful attempt to write a screenplay based on the life of Malcolm X, he began immediately to sob, "more in a helpless rage," he told Weatherby, "than in sorrow."

King's death nearly destroyed him. "Circumstances, if not temperament," had prevented genuine friendship between them, Baldwin wrote of King, but his "respect and affection" for the civil rights leader had been great, and he despaired when he considered what the slain leader's death meant for America. Riots engulfed the country following King's murder, as blacks struck out in their own helpless rage; the most beloved proponent of nonviolence had been killed, and in a strange way, violence suddenly made sense to people who had turned the other cheek for years. No other event had come so close to inducing Baldwin to succumb to the bitterness and despair that he had so long ago dedicated his life to overcoming; King's murder would force him, in *No Name in the Street,* to a reconsideration and restatement of the challenge—between acceptance "of life as it is, and men as they are," and opposition to injustice—he had laid out for himself many years before in the concluding paragraphs of *Notes of a Native Son*: "Perhaps even more than the death itself, the manner of his death had forced me into a judgment concerning human life and human beings which I have always been reluctant to make. . . . Incontestably, alas, most people are not worth very much; and yet, every human being is an unprecedented miracle."

"Much of his hope died with King," said Baldwin's close friend, the actor Billy Dee Williams, at whose home the writer had been when he learned of the assassination; other friends, such as Kenneth Clark and Bayard Rustin, spoke similarly about the change in Baldwin following the tragedy. Age seemed to take hold of him overnight, his already heavy drinking increased even more, and he often resorted to tranquilizers to get to sleep. His grief and frustration were palpable; always fond of intelligent debate, he was now often argumentative and strident in conversation and sometimes made intemperate remarks in interview settings, as when he told a questioner that he believed it quite likely that white America was engaging in an organized extermination of blacks akin to the Holocaust. For a time, he was unable to write at all; for the rest of his life, writing would remain extremely difficult for him. Grieving and deeply anguished, he left the country once more, not long after King's funeral. Never again would he make the United States his home.

CHAPTER EIGHT

HOPE
IS INVENTED
EVERY DAY

Baldwin in his Istanbul flat
in December 1969. The
months following King's
assassination were some
of the darkest days he had
known: "I didn't think I could
write at all. I didn't see any
point to it. I was hurt. . . .
I can't even talk about it.
I didn't know how to continue,
couldn't see my way clear."

Baldwin went first to Paris, but he had become as famous in France as he was in America, and once again he found himself besieged by fans and reporters. Now even in Istanbul the press sought him out. He tried to hide there and even directed a few plays, but he could not write and his physical condition was not good. "I want a place where I can find out again where I am, and what I must do," he said. "A place where I can stop and do nothing in order to start again." But Istanbul was not that place, and soon he was on the move again, to London, and Italy, and back to Paris. He was, wrote a reporter who visited him at this time, "awash in a special sort of aloneness" and seemed "infinitely older than anyone else one knows." Though he expressed the belief that one must always remain hopeful, he was afraid that the civil rights movement had died with King.

The breakneck pace of his last several years caught up with him, and grief and exhaustion, aggravated by late hours and heavy drinking, brought about a physical and nervous collapse on several occasions. In Paris, in 1970, he was hospitalized for 10 days; when he was released, friends brought him to recuperate to the tiny, picturesque village of Saint-Paul-de-Vence in Provence, in the south of France, about 10 miles from the port city of Nice. Though he did not realize it immediately, Baldwin, at age 47, had found his home. After staying in a hotel for a time, he rented a room in a 300-year-old, 12-room farmhouse set on 12 acres of rambling gardens and ancient trees, with an incomparable view of the mountains and a valley that descended to the Côte d'Azur. Soon, to house the family members and friends who seemed always to be visiting, he was renting virtually every room in the house, and he eventually decided to buy it.

He was criticized, of course, for his decision to expatriate himself once again, asked time and time again how someone who considered himself an activist could live at such a remove from his people and the struggle. "I could say, you know, that I have found a haven, although I know very well that that's not true," he told an interviewer from the *Black Scholar* in 1973. "I am *not* in exile and I am *not* in paradise. It rains down here too." He continued to keep abreast of events in the United States and to lend support, in the form of public statements, time, and sometimes money, to causes, both political and personal, that seemed to him worthwhile. The arrests of Stokely Carmichael and the California educator and activist Angela Davis, for example, provoked Baldwin to defend them in print, and he devoted an enormous amount of time and money to a seven-year crusade to secure the freedom of Tony Maynard, a friend and former assistant, who had been falsely convicted of murder. To a reporter from *Life* magazine, he intimated that his retreat was but a brief hiatus before he returned to the fray: "I am in calculation. . . . That means I'm plotting something."

The results of that plotting were not immediately evident in the form of new literary output. Baldwin had always been a provocative conversationalist, and his next two published books were transcripts of long dialogues on race and other issues between himself and Margaret

Mead, the esteemed anthropologist, and between himself and Nikki Giovanni, the young black poet. Though interesting in many regards, *A Rap on Race,* which was published in 1971, and *A Dialogue,* published the following year, did nothing to stem the erosion of his reputation as a literary figure. The long, rambling memoir *No Name in the Street,* a reflection on his years in the civil rights movement and the death of King, was a much more significant and substantial piece of work, but it was not much more well received than any of his recent projects. Responding to Baldwin's declaration that he had surrendered hope that white America would ever live up to the moral challenge of providing justice for black citizens, critics accused him of sacrificing his literary

Baldwin onstage at a London lecture. In the last years of his life, he came to regard the imparting of his experience through university lectures as increasingly important. "The only way to teach history is to make them go through it themselves," he said of his students.

voice and artistic integrity to the propaganda of political extremism, of succumbing finally to bitterness and hatred. The essay echoed, in places, the apocalyptic tone of *The Fire Next Time,* but to many readers Baldwin's rhetoric seemed tired, drained of its originality and Biblical fervor. Though his message had become more extreme—he likened the United States to a "Fourth Reich" and proclaimed that he had no compassion for his country or his countrymen—his words, curiously, seemed to lack conviction.

Disheartened by the reviews, increasingly unsure of himself as a writer, Baldwin "didn't know for a long time whether I wanted to keep on writing or not," but he decided to persevere, inspired, he said, by the example of King. "What I said to myself was that Martin never stopped. So I can't either. It was as painful as that." He now regarded himself, he often said, as the "last witness" to the heroic struggles of the 1960s, equating himself with King and Malcolm X and Medgar Evers and even John and Robert Kennedy, all of them murdered. Always fond of self-dramatization, he told friends that he had, before he left the United States, sometimes feared that he would be next.

Inspired by the mistreatment of his friend Tony Maynard by the American criminal-justice system, the plot of Baldwin's next novel, *If Beale Street Could Talk,* which was published in 1974, concerns a young black man—Alonzo, called Fonny, a sculptor—accused of a crime he did not commit and confined in New York City's infamous Tombs detention center. The book is narrated by Clementine, called Tish, his fiancée, who learns shortly after his imprisonment that she is pregnant with their child and works, despite her lack of money and resources, to secure his release. It was a situation that Baldwin had explored before: in *Go Tell It on the Mountain,* he had "solved" fictionally the mystery of his biological father's identity by ascribing the paternity of John Grimes to a handsome, sensitive, intelligent man named Richard, who commits suicide after being badly beaten in prison following a white merchant's false accusation of robbery. The situation in *If Beale Street Could Talk* differs significantly in that the accuser, unlike the victimized but still malicious white man in *Go Tell It on the Mountain,* is Puerto Rican and sincerely mistaken; culpability for Fonny's imprisonment rests primarily with a corrupt and racist police officer—that is, not with a private citizen, but, as Baldwin portrays it, with the representative of an institution and system that operates specifically to destroy blacks— and there is at least the implication that Fonny survives his ordeal.

As with all of Baldwin's best work, the novel presents an almost overwhelming argument to justify great bitterness and even hatred, and overcomes it with an almost illogical, tenuous, yet undeniable message of hope, represented in this instance by the birth of a child: not hope born of the unrealistic optimism that comes from the unwillingness to face the truth, but the hope that is born from, as Baldwin put it in *The Fire Next Time,* "continually surviving the worst that life can bring" and facing the knowledge, forced upon blacks by their history in this country and avoided at all costs by whites, that "life is tragic." Critical opinions on the novel were as sharply divided as the two contradictions Baldwin had sought to balance throughout his artistic and personal life. *If Beale Street Could Talk* was either Baldwin's "best novel yet" or "insipid" and "slight"; Baldwin himself was either at the height of his powers as the creator of a "timeless" work of art or had become a "dated" relic most interesting as a nostalgia piece.

Once again, it seemed, Baldwin had found a way to get past bitterness and despair. Resigned to the fact that he was unlikely to return to critical favor in the near future, he discovered nevertheless a renewed commitment to writing and planned a number of ambitious literary projects, among them a work—a novel about a gospel singer—that had been in progress for several years and would eventually be published as *Just Above My Head* and another, as yet less clearly defined novel, with the working title of *No Papers for Mohammed. The Devil Finds Work,* a memoir of sorts in the form of criticism of films he had seen at various points in his life, appeared in 1976, as did *Little Man, Little Man,* a children's story. Despite fairly frequent trips to New York City, for business and to visit friends and family, and elsewhere in the United States to give lectures and speeches, he had come to regard Saint-Paul-de-Vence as home. In France, he was seldom alone; a succession of attractive young men from diverse backgrounds moved through his life for weeks and sometimes months on end. None gave him the permanence he still sometimes claimed to be looking for in a relationship (and friends still often described him as lonely), but his social life seemed nonetheless to sustain him. Relatives, such as his brother David, and old and dear friends, such as Lucien, were frequently in residence at the farmhouse, and Baldwin enjoyed the respect and admiration of the people of the village, who were zealous in guarding his privacy. Though he had caustically described himself in print just a few years earlier (in

At a press conference in Los Angeles, California, in February 1985, Baldwin issued a warning about conditions in the south-central section of the city, where seven years later savage rioting would occur following the acquittal of several white policemen for the beating of a black man.

No Name in the Street) as an "aging, lonely, sexually dubious, politically outrageous, unspeakably erratic freak," he now seemed more at peace with himself, and more willing, as in the past, to concede the possibility of good in the world. His own time, he seemed to sense, was passing; though there was still much he wished to say, it was nearing time to hand on the struggle to someone else. "I know that my great-nieces and great-nephews are living in a different world than the world in which I was born," he told an interviewer in the late 1970s. "They can not imagine the world which produced me, but I've seen the world for which they are going to be responsible. . . . And I trust them to do it . . . . There's no reason to despair. . . . I'm far from being in despair. We cannot afford despair. We have too many children. Despair is a luxury only white men can afford."

He began now to devote an increasingly large amount of time to university speaking and lecturing, using his own experience to educate the young people to whom his generation would ultimately have to entrust the world. "People are very critical and very despairing of the young," he told an interviewer in 1979, "but I must say that my experience in all these years on campus has given me a great deal of hope. Kids ask real questions." That year, Morehouse University, a traditionally black college and the alma mater of Martin Luther King, awarded Baldwin an honorary doctorate.

That same year, Dial Press published Baldwin's last novel, *Just Above My Head,* the life story, narrated as reminiscence by his brother Hall, of Arthur Montana, a gay, extremely successful gospel singer. Baldwin's longest novel by far, *Just Above My Head* encompassed much of its author's experience, as, through the characters of Hall and Arthur, he returned to the storefront churches and drenching religiosity of the Harlem of his youth, his days as a black expatriate in France, the harrowing trips through the South in the cause of civil rights, the ambiguous rewards of fame and stardom. In *Just Above My Head,* Baldwin writes about sex between men more straightforwardly than ever he had before, about love between adults more hopefully, and about first love—in this case, between boys—more joyfully. Though deeply skeptical about organized religion of the kind to which Baldwin was exposed as a youth, the novel is nonetheless suffused with the music of the black church, spirituals and gospel songs, as well as with the blues (especially of Bessie Smith and Ma Rainey) and jazz, all the songs of sorrow that Baldwin had come to regard as the most important artistic legacy of the African American experience.

"Niggers can sing gospel," Hall Montana, the novel's narrator explains (note the assumption that he is speaking to a fellow black), "as no other people can because they aren't singing gospel. . . . When a nigger quotes the Gospel, he is not quoting; he is telling you what happened to him today, and what is certainly going to happen to you tomorrow." One of the members of Arthur Montana's quartet sings the words to a spiritual about Mary and Joseph and the baby Jesus finding no room at the inn, and Hall continues: "He was not singing about a road in Egypt two thousand years ago, but about his mama and his daddy and himself, and those streets just outside, brother, just outside of every door, those streets which you and I both walk and which we are going to walk until we meet." In his last novel, Baldwin had finally succeeded in achieving his goal of using his literary voice to achieve the prose equivalent of the songs of sorrow he so greatly admired.

"[Blacks] brought themselves a long way out of bondage by means of the music which *Just Above My Head* is at bottom about," he told Wolfgang Binder in an interview in 1980. "So in a sense the novel is a kind of return to my own beginnings, which are not only mine, and a way of using that beginning to start again. In my own mind I come full circle from *Go Tell It on the Mountain* to *Just Above My Head*." As if to emphasize the notion of a "return to beginnings" and having come "full circle," he dedicated the novel to his three brothers and five sisters, to all of whom he had remained extremely close.

Though the novel would be Baldwin's first commercial success in nearly 15 years—it spent 37 weeks on the *Washington Post* best-seller list, became a featured alternate selection of the Book-of-the-Month Club, and garnered Baldwin an impressive $305,000 for the paperback rights—it marked less an opportunity to start again than an ending. He would publish no more new fiction, and his work time was spent increasingly in looks backward. He lectured at the University of

California on the civil rights movement, and in 1981 a documentary producer filmed him as he paid visits to the sites of major events from the heyday of the movement and reminisced with old comrades and friends from those years. Aggravated by drinking and irregular hours, his health continued to be poor, and he was hospitalized on several occasions. Friends who had not seen him in a while were usually surprised, upon their meeting again, by how old he looked. During a stint in the early 1980s as a guest lecturer at five colleges affiliated with the University of Massachusetts, he was noted to be drinking heavily and had to be hospitalized after suffering a mild heart attack; doctor's orders to curtail his drinking and smoking and get more sleep went unheeded. He spoke often to a friend of his loneliness, though he seemed never to lack for young male companions. At a 60th birthday party held for him in Amherst, Massachusetts, he was honored by such distinguished guests as the writer Maya Angelou and the historian Lerone Bennett. "I've learned one thing," Baldwin said at the close of the ceremony to those who had come to honor him. "Never avoid the truth about yourself."

That truth, he continued to teach, resided in an individuality far more unique, valuable, and complex than any reductive labels, such as skin color or sexual preference, could contain. The challenge for the new generation of black writers, Baldwin told Julius Lester, a colleague at the University of Massachusetts, continued to be "to make the question of color obsolete." Lester replied that many of these younger black writers believed it was their duty to write only about black people, but Baldwin, whose last two novels had not featured any major white characters, saw no discord between the two positions. "That is not a conflict," he told Lester. "If our voices are heard, it makes the concept of color obsolete. That has to be its inevitable result."

He also continued to regard sexual labels as inadequate representations of his experience and identity. Neither the word "homosexual" nor "gay," he continued to insist, defined or described him. In the course of a 1984 interview with Baldwin, Richard Goldstein of the *Village Voice* asked him, "Is it problematic for you, the idea of having sex only with other people who are identified as gay?"

Clergy conduct the funeral service for
Baldwin at the Cathedral of St. John the
Divine in New York City on December 8, 1987.

"The people who were my lovers," Baldwin replied, "were never, well, the word gay wouldn't have meant anything to them."

"They moved in the straight world?" Goldstein persisted.

"They moved in the world," Baldwin replied.

"I've loved a few men and I've loved a few women" was Baldwin's most frequent response to those who asked him about his homosexuality. He was ambivalent about the gay rights movement, which did not interest him very much. "As regards . . . gay liberation," he told an interviewer a few years before his death, "I'm very glad that it seems to be easier for a boy to admit that he's in love with a boy, or for a girl to admit that she's in love with a girl," but on other occasions he dismissed the gay rights movement as essentially a white, middle-class

At an outdoor café in the French village of Saint-Paul-de-Vence in April 1985, the sixty-one-year-old Baldwin looks at his first novel, *Go Tell It on the Mountain.* "I know we can be better than we are," he had told an interviewer the previous year. "That's the sum total of my wisdom in all these years. . . . There're two things we have to do—love each other and raise our children."

phenomenon that was "not really one of my prime concerns." Often, he referred to the movement as a "club," usually adding, "I have not really got to join a club in order to go to bed with a man or fall in love." His sexual identity, he told Goldstein, was "really a matter between me

and God," and was nobody's business but his own. "There is nothing in me," he said, "that is not in everybody else"; each of us, he maintained in the essay "Here Be Dragons," written near the end of his life, is essentially androgynous: "each of us, helplessly and forever, contains the other—male in female, female in male, white in black, and black in white. We are a part of each other."

Baldwin's last original book, *The Evidence of Things Not Seen,* was published in 1985. The book was an expanded version of an essay he had originally written for *Playboy* magazine in 1981 about a series of murders of black children in Atlanta, Georgia; a young black man, Wayne Williams, had been convicted of the crime, but many people, Baldwin among them, retained doubts about his guilt and the fairness of the judicial proceedings through which he was convicted. The book's publication marked the end of his long relationship with Dial Press, which had rejected his manuscript; in truth the long essay, though deeply felt, never approached the brilliance he had brought to the form in such pieces as "Notes of a Native Son" and "Down at the Cross." Straightforward reporting was never Baldwin's strength; he was better at using events to trigger his own thoughts and feelings, as a jumping-off point for a journey of exploration into his own conscious-ness, and the events and truths of the Williams trial proved too tangled for him to unravel or to stimulate new insight into the state of race relations in the United States.

Baldwin's final book, *The Price of the Ticket,* was also published in 1985. The book was a collection of every one of his essays, arranged in chronological order. At the time, *The Price of the Ticket* was largely ignored by the critics or condemned with faint praise as a historical curiosity, but to look at it now is to marvel anew at the literary evidence of a lifetime spent in passionate, honest, and intelligent search for the truth. And if this native son seemed without honor in his own land, France was more appreciative. In 1986, François Mitterand, the president of Baldwin's adopted country, invested the black American writer as a Commander of the Legion d'Honneur, one of France's most treasured awards.

Just months later, Baldwin learned he had cancer of the esophagus. An operation was performed, without much success, and through the spring and summer months of 1987, as he rested at the farmhouse in Saint-Paul-de-Vence, he grew steadily weaker. He died on December 1, attended, as he had been throughout his illness, by his brother David, Lucien Happersberger, and Bernard Hassell, a longtime friend who had served as his secretary since the late 1960s. His last request had been to be propped up in bed so that he could see the mountains.

A week later at the Cathedral of St. John the Divine in New York City, only a number of blocks from where he was born, 5,000 mourners came to wish him farewell at what was officially termed a celebration, complete with spirituals and jazz and a recording of the author reading the prayer "Precious Lord." Writers and musicians and famous friends—poets Amiri Baraka and Maya Angelou, novelists Toni Morrison, Paule Marshall, and William Styron, jazz drummer Max Roach—paid him tribute with their attendance, as did thousands of less well-known Americans whose lives he had touched with his work and presence. In a brief written remembrance distributed by the family at the service to honor "that smile, those eyes, that strong hand of our son, our brother, our uncle, our father," his many surviving relatives likened his work to a song, "more like a blues than a hymn," sung in a "sorrowful, triumphant, biblical" voice that exposed "all attempts to organize human society which violate the society of the human heart." That song, they wrote, had a constant refrain: "Love is a battle, love is war, love is growing up."

BOOKS BY JAMES BALDWIN

FURTHER READING

Bloom, Harold, ed. *James Baldwin*. New York: Chelsea House, 1986.

Branch, Taylor. *Parting the Waters: America in the King Years*. New York: Simon and Schuster, 1989.

Campbell, James. *Talking at the Gates: A Life of James Baldwin*. New York: Viking, 1991.

Eckman, Fern Marja. *The Furious Passage of James Baldwin*. New York: Evans, 1966.

O'Daniel, Therman B., ed. *James Baldwin: A Critical Evaluation*. Washington, D.C.: Howard University Press, 1977.

Standley, Fred L., and Louis H. Pratt, eds. *Conversations with James Baldwin*. Jackson: University Press of Mississippi, 1989.

Troupe, Quincy, ed. *James Baldwin: The Legacy*. New York: Touchstone/Simon and Schuster, 1989.

Walker, Margaret. *Richard Wright: Daemonic Genius: A Portrait of the Man, a Critical Look at His Work*. New York: Warner Books, 1988.

Weatherby, James J. *James Baldwin: Artist on Fire*. New York: Donald I. Fine, 1989.

Williams, Juan. *Eyes on the Prize: America's Civil Rights Years*. New York: Viking, 1987.

CHRONOLOGY

1924   James Arthur Baldwin born on August 2 in Harlem,
        New York, to Emma Berdis Jones

1927   Marriage of mother to David Baldwin

1936–37 Baldwin studies with poet Countee Cullen
        at Frederick Douglass Junior High School

1938   Becomes a Young Minister at the Fireside Pentecostal
        Assembly in Harlem

1942   Graduates from De Witt Clinton High School;
        renounces the ministry; begins work on a series of
        menial jobs

1943   David Baldwin dies on July 29

1945   Baldwin meets novelist Richard Wright

1947   First professional publication, the review "Maxim
        Gorky as Artist," appears in the *Nation* magazine

1948   Baldwin leaves for Paris, France, on November 11

1949   Meets Lucien Happersberger

1953   *Go Tell It on the Mountain* published to critical praise

1954   Completes first play, *The Amen Corner*

1955   Baldwin's first book of nonfiction, *Notes of a Native
        Son,* published

1956   *Giovanni's Room,* groundbreaking novel about
        homosexuality, published

1957   Visits the American South for the first time; writes
        first essays on the civil rights movement for *Harper's*
        and *Partisan Review*

1961   Second collection of essays, *Nobody Knows My Name,*
        published

1962	*Another Country,* best-selling novel, published; Baldwin travels to Africa; meets the Honorable Elijah Muhammad of the Nation of Islam
1963	*The Fire Next Time* published; Baldwin awarded the George Polk Memorial Award for magazine reporting; meets with U.S. attorney general Robert F. Kennedy
1964	*Blues for Mister Charlie* opens on Broadway; *Nothing Personal* published; Baldwin elected to the National Institute of Arts and Letters
1965	*The Amen Corner* produced on Broadway; *Going to Meet the Man,* a collection of short stories, published
1968	Publication of the novel *Tell Me How Long the Train's Been Gone* and the play *The Amen Corner*
1971	*A Rap on Race,* with anthropologist Margaret Mead, published
1972	*No Name in the Street,* an essay on the civil rights movement, and *One Day, When I Was Lost,* an unproduced screenplay about the life of Malcolm X, published
1973	Publication of *A Dialogue* with the poet and activist, Nikki Giovanni
1974	Publication of fifth novel, *If Beale Street Could Talk*
1976	Awarded honorary doctorate from Morehouse College
1979	Publication of last novel, *Just Above My Head*
1982	Awarded honorary doctorate from the City University of New York
1985	Publication of *The Price of the Ticket: Collected Nonfiction, 1948–1985*
1986	Awarded the Commander of the Legion d'Honneur by France's president, François Mitterrand
1987	Dies on December 1 in St. Paul-de-Vence; funeral on December 8 at the Cathedral of St. John the Divine in New York City

INDEX

Randall Kenan was born in Brooklyn, New York, in 1963 and grew up in Chinquapin, North Carolina. He received a bachelor's degree in English at the University of North Carolina and is currently teaching English at Sarah Lawrence College. His first novel, *A Visitation of Spirits,* was published in 1989 to great acclaim. His second book, *Let the Dead Bury Their Dead,* was nominated for the 1993 National Book Critics Circle Award and won a Lambda Award for best gay men's fiction.

Martin Duberman is Distinguished Professor of History at the Graduate Center for the City University of New York and the founder and director of the Center for Gay and Lesbian Studies. One of the country's foremost historians, he is the author of 14 books and numerous articles and essays. He has won the Bancroft Prize for *Charles Francis Adams* (1960); two Lambda awards for *Hidden from History: Reclaiming the Gay and Lesbian Past,* an anthology that he coedited; and a special award from the National Academy of Arts and Letters for his overall "contributions to literature." His play *In White America* won the Vernon Rice/Drama Desk Award in 1964. His other works include *James Russell Lowell* (1966), *Black Mountain: An Exploration in Community* (1972), *Paul Robeson* (1989), *Cures: A Gay Man's Odyssey* (1991), and *Stonewall* (1993).

Professor Duberman received his Ph.D. in history from Harvard University in 1957 and served as professor of history at Yale University and Princeton University from 1957 until 1972, when he assumed his present position at the City University of New York.